Cambridge Elements

Elements in the Aegean Bronze Age
edited by
Carl Knappett
University of Toronto
Irene Nikolakopoulou
Hellenic Ministry of Culture, Archaeological Museum of Heraklion

THE EMERGENCE OF AEGEAN PREHISTORY

Andrew Shapland
University of Oxford

Shaftesbury Road, Cambridge CB2 8EA, United Kingdom

One Liberty Plaza, 20th Floor, New York, NY 10006, USA

477 Williamstown Road, Port Melbourne, VIC 3207, Australia

314–321, 3rd Floor, Plot 3, Splendor Forum, Jasola District Centre,
New Delhi – 110025, India

103 Penang Road, #05–06/07, Visioncrest Commercial, Singapore 238467

Cambridge University Press is part of Cambridge University Press & Assessment,
a department of the University of Cambridge.

We share the University's mission to contribute to society through the pursuit of
education, learning and research at the highest international levels of excellence.

www.cambridge.org
Information on this title: www.cambridge.org/9781009670883

DOI: 10.1017/9781009342889

© Andrew Shapland 2025

This publication is in copyright. Subject to statutory exception and to the provisions
of relevant collective licensing agreements, no reproduction of any part may take
place without the written permission of Cambridge University Press & Assessment.

When citing this work, please include a reference to the DOI 10.1017/9781009342889

First published 2025

A catalogue record for this publication is available from the British Library

ISBN 978-1-009-67088-3 Hardback
ISBN 978-1-009-34284-1 Paperback
ISSN 2754-2998 (online)
ISSN 2754-298X (print)

Cambridge University Press & Assessment has no responsibility for the persistence
or accuracy of URLs for external or third-party internet websites referred to in this
publication and does not guarantee that any content on such websites is, or will
remain, accurate or appropriate.

For EU product safety concerns, contact us at Calle de José Abascal, 56, 1°, 28003
Madrid, Spain, or email eugpsr@cambridge.org

The Emergence of Aegean Prehistory

Elements in the Aegean Bronze Age

DOI: 10.1017/9781009342889
First published online: March 2025

Andrew Shapland
University of Oxford

Author for correspondence: Andrew Shapland,
andrew.shapland@ashmus.ox.ac.uk

Abstract: This Element focusses on the emergence of Aegean Prehistory as a discipline, starting with the first recorded encounters with prehistoric monuments and artefacts and ending with the decipherment of Linear B in 1952. It broadens the history of Aegean Bronze Age archaeology as told in popular accounts as a series of excavations of great men, particularly Heinrich Schliemann at Troy and Mycenae and Sir Arthur Evans at Knossos. Though their work is of fundamental importance for the discipline, here it is placed within wider political, institutional and intellectual frameworks. This Element also provides an overview of the work of many other archaeologists across the Aegean and the regional and historical context in which they operated. It provides a brief but comprehensive history of the formative stages of the study of Aegean Prehistory.

Keywords: Minoan, Mycenaean, Aegean Bronze Age, Cycladic, history of archaeology

© Andrew Shapland 2025

ISBNs: 9781009670883 (HB), 9781009342841 (PB), 9781009342889 (OC)
ISSNs: 2754-2998 (online), 2754-298X (print)

Contents

1 Introduction 1

2 Biographical Framework 4

3 Intellectual Context 8

4 Political and Institutional History of Archaeology in the Aegean 17

5 History of Archaeological Research in the Aegean 25

6 Broadening Aegean Prehistory 66

References 69

1 Introduction

Few books on the history of archaeology fail to mention Heinrich Schliemann's excavations at Troy and Mycenae or Sir Arthur Evans' work at Knossos. These men are often cast as pioneers, opening up new vistas for archaeology in general and Aegean Prehistory in particular. Their personalities tend to receive more attention than the complicated historical and intellectual contexts in which the excavation of these sites became possible or even thinkable. The more simplistic accounts credit them with the discovery of these sites, ignoring the local inhabitants and travellers who recognised and explored these places before them. Nor did these founding figures excavate their sites single-handedly, but rather employed teams of hundreds of diggers, pot-washers and assistants. Once their excavation campaigns had finished, others continued to survey and excavate, resulting in a cumulative understanding of these sites. Their contemporaries, particularly those who did not publish their finds in German, English, French or Italian, are often marginalised. Any history of the subject is inevitably selective but the choice of names of people and places matters when describing the emergence of Aegean Prehistory. In order to understand the emergence of this body of knowledge, it is important to recognise that these names stand for a much richer set of engagements with the material traces of the past.

One of the first histories of Aegean Prehistory, published before Evans began excavating Knossos, was written by another renowned archaeologist, Christos Tsountas. His summary of the emerging discipline was first published in Greek in 1893, followed by an expanded English translation in 1897: *The Mycenaean Age: A Study of the Monuments and Culture of Pre-Homeric Greece* (Tsountas 1893; Tsountas and Manatt 1897). There, in a brief introduction, he gave an account of the first twenty years of the discipline as a sequence of the excavation of sites and the names of their excavators. Although, as he acknowledged, sites like Mycenae and Tiryns were described by ancient Greek historians and had never disappeared, he argued that Heinrich Schliemann's excavations of the Shaft Graves at Mycenae in 1876 nevertheless marked a horizon for the study of the Bronze Age. Deploying a metaphor which frequently recurs in narratives of this kind, he suggested that it was at this time that 'the first clear light broke forth' (Tsountas and Manatt 1897: 4).

As discoveries accumulated in the twentieth century, Aegean prehistorians started to write about the history of their subject (Myres 1933;

Stubbings 1972). Both William McDonald's (1967) *Progress into the Past* and Lesley Fitton's (1995) *The Discovery of the Greek Bronze Age* opt for 1870 as a key juncture, the first year of Schliemann's excavations at Troy. Both also highlight the importance of the decipherment of Linear B in 1952 as a pivotal moment. The revelation that the Linear B tablets found at Knossos and Pylos preserved an early form of Greek helped to strengthen the traditional ties between Aegean Prehistory and the Homeric epics which had long offered a quasi-historical background to the archaeological discoveries. At the same time it partially resolved a decades-long debate about the timing of the 'arrival of the Greeks' which had entangled the archaeological discoveries in questions of culture, race and language.

This Element also takes 1952 as a cut-off point for the emergence of Aegean Prehistory. This year also marked the resumption of excavations at Pylos following the disruption of the Second World War and the Greek Civil War that immediately succeeded it. It is a reminder that archaeology does not operate independently of political history, something that will be emphasised here. As Ian Morris (1994) has suggested, disciplinary histories of classical archaeology can be divided into 'internalist' accounts which focus on the sequence of discoveries and interpretative frameworks and 'externalist' accounts which seek to embed these in wider historical developments. These developments are not just political but also intellectual. Debates over the 'Antiquity of Man' and evolution in the nineteenth century challenged biblical narratives of humanity's history as human origins were pushed back into geological time.

Identifying a starting point for the emergence of Aegean Prehistory is more problematic. Since surveys and excavations of what is now recognised as prehistoric material go back at least as far as the early nineteenth century, it is difficult to pinpoint the origin of the discipline. Most scholars, however, would place the emergence of archaeology as a discipline in the nineteenth century, tied up with modernity (Schnapp 1996: 275; Thomas 2004: 2). Identifying a specific starting point such as 1870 establishes Heinrich Schliemann as the founding figure of the discipline at the same time as excluding the numerous scholars who had studied, and even excavated, Troy, Mycenae and Tiryns before him. Another problem with origins is that disciplinary histories tend to fall into a narrative of continuous progress, making the contingent and accidental seem inevitable (Fotiadis 2017). Lying behind metaphors of light and darkness are notions of gradual enlightenment as each new discovery comes out of the ground, starting with the discoveries at Troy or Mycenae.

Another problem comes from trying to distinguish archaeological excavation or survey from what are essentially the same activities undertaken by local inhabitants or eighteenth-century travellers. Yannis Hamilakis (2011: 49) criticises 'a linear, developmental, evolutionist narrative for the discipline'. By defining archaeology in terms of material engagement with traces of the past, Hamilakis opens the way for what he terms 'indigenous archaeologies'. This provides an important counterpoint to official, disciplinary histories by examining how local populations understood the same sites and objects. It is an approach which he identifies as 'postcolonial' although, as he acknowledges, the political history of what are now Greece and Turkey complicates this label (Hamilakis 2008). Aegean Prehistory emerged at a time of shifting borders as the Ottoman Empire disintegrated and the Greek nation expanded, with the 'Great Powers' always ready to intervene. This provided the legal and political framework within which these material engagements could take place.

Against this backdrop, this Element will provide an outline which complicates the familiar narrative of Aegean Prehistory as a gradual accumulation of knowledge about the past. It starts by reviewing the 'internalist' biographical approach to Aegean prehistorians before providing aspects of an 'externalist' approach which sets out the political and intellectual context in which archaeologists were working. Following this is an account of archaeological work in different regions of the Aegean which emphasises their different historical contexts but also their different materialities (Figure 1). Rather than cumulative moments in the history of Aegean Bronze Age archaeology, each excavation is an act of material engagement between an archaeologist and an assemblage of things from the past which takes place within a particular spatial and historical framework. Archaeologists can be defined as people who participate in archaeological institutions such as learned societies and their associated publications. The history of Aegean Prehistory is derived from the translation of excavations and finds into words and images. Although it is convenient to describe this history in terms of relationships between excavators and sites, it is important to remember that this is a two-way relationship. The materiality of sites and artefacts shape the stories that can be told about them. If there is a uniting theme in the history of the discipline it is that objects and sites endure, while the stories that are told about them change.

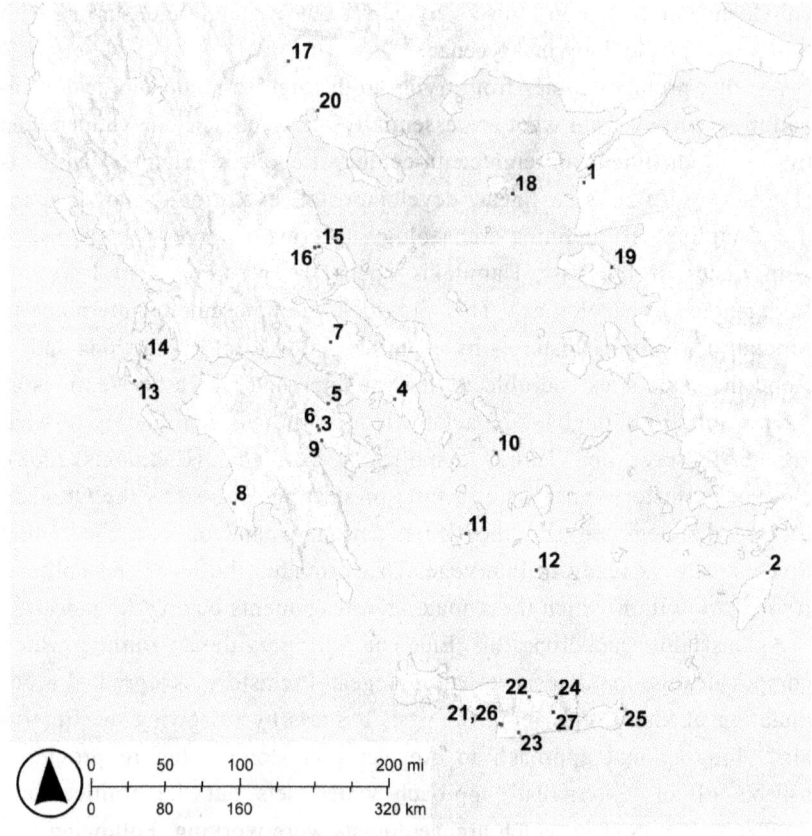

Figure 1 Key sites discussed in the text by region: Troad: 1. Troy; Dodecanese: 2. Ialysos; Peloponnese and Central Greece: 3. Argive Heraion, 4. Athens, 5. Korakou, 6. Mycenae, 7. Orchomenos, 8. Pylos, 9. Tiryns; Cycladic Islands: 10. Chalandriani, 11. Phylakopi, 12. Therasia; Ionian Islands: 13. Alalkomenes, 14. Mazarakata; Thessaly: 15. Dimini, 16. Sesklo; Northern Greece and the Islands of the Northern Aegean: 17. Chauchitza, 18. Poliochni, 19. Thermi, 20. Toumba Thessaloniki; Crete: 21. Ayia Triada, 22. Knossos, 23. Koumasa, 24. Mallia, 25. Palaikastro, 26. Phaistos, 27. Psychro.

2 Biographical Framework

One of Heinrich Schliemann's contributions to Aegean Prehistory was to establish the archaeologist as a romantic hero. His first works, including the first volume of his excavations at Troy, took the form of diaries, prefaced with an autobiographical sketch (Schliemann 1869, 1875). The effect was to present his archaeological research as a quest with himself as the protagonist. Even the more scientific *Ilios*, whose chapters outline the strata of Troy one by one, begins with an expanded autobiographical section. In it the young Schliemann argues with his father about whether the Trojan War happened and resolves to discover the truth by excavating Troy (Schliemann 1880: 3). Its purpose was to establish his excavations as a fulfilment of destiny, realising his childhood dreams of excavating Troy and finding the truth in Homer despite various setbacks along the way. This approach was consolidated by Karl Schuchhardt (1891), who published a narrative of Schliemann's career as an archaeologist which also summarised the results of his research. A later official biography characterised him as a gold-seeker and declared that 'everything about him was romantic, the kings whose treasures he unearthed, the others who bestowed treasures upon him' (Ludwig 1931: v). For a century this account of the archaeologist-hero was unquestioningly retold in various biographies and histories of archaeology before doubts started to emerge about its veracity on the 150th anniversary of his birth (Calder 1972). Although there had always been doubts about Schliemann's archaeological claims, particularly when they were based on his literal reading of Homer, his later critics regarded him as a fraud, and even a psychopath (Calder and Trail 1986; Traill 1995). Rather than undermine Schliemann's importance, however, this debate only serves to reinforce his role as the prime mover in Aegean Prehistory. His 200th anniversary saw another conference and publication (Laffineur and Perna 2024).

In some ways the reception of Sir Arthur Evans' career has been similar. His excavations at Knossos began in 1900, over a decade after Schliemann had tried to gain the rights to excavate there. A biography by Arthur's half-sister, Joan Evans, provided a largely uncritical account of his life and discoveries which acted as a source for numerous other accounts (Evans 1943; Cottrell 1955, Horwitz 1981). A leitmotif of her book is revealed by its title, *Time and Chance*, which at times is invoked as an explanation for her brother's discoveries:

> He had set out to find a script; he had found four and could read none of them. But Time and Chance had made him the discoverer of a new civilization, and he had to make it intelligible to other men. Fortunately it was exactly to his taste: set in beautiful Mediterranean country, aristocratic and humane in feeling; creating an art brilliant in colour and unusual in form, that drew inspiration from the flowers and birds and creatures that he loved. (Evans 1943: 350)

A more recent biography by Alexander MacGillivray (2000), timed to mark the centenary of the excavations at Knossos, suggested instead that Evans had created the Minoans out of his imagination. This was a contribution to a wider debate about whether Evans' vision of the Minoans and his reconstructions at Knossos were based on a fantasy (Farnoux 1993; Papadopoulos 2005; D'Agata 2010; Schoep 2018). Nevertheless, Evans still has his defenders (Warren 2000; Marinatos 2014).

The significance of the biographical approach for the history of Aegean Prehistory does not lie in the truth or otherwise of claims made about Heinrich Schliemann and Sir Arthur Evans. It is important because it provides one of the dominant frameworks for understanding Aegean Prehistory, which has been dubbed the 'Great Men of Archaeology' genre (Moshenska and Lewis 2023: 2). It places the excavators themselves at the centre of the narrative, overlooking the collaborative nature of both excavations and scholarship. In his history of classical archaeology in Greece, Paul MacKendrick uses Schliemann as an archetypal excavator, suggesting that 'If Knossos shares with Troy the glamor among prehistoric sites in the Aegean basin, it is because it, like Troy, was excavated by a rich and flamboyant character, Sir Arthur Evans' (MacKendrick 1962: 46). McDonald's *Progress into the Past* is structured by the lives of the leading Homeric archaeologists of three generations, Schliemann, Evans and a third 'pioneer', Carl Blegen. McDonald, a colleague of Blegen's at Pylos, argued that what they have in common is that 'They seem to possess a special blend of brilliance, self-assurance, intuition and luck' (McDonald 1967: xv).

One of the problems with the biographical approach is that it establishes archaeological sites and objects as passive entities, on which excavators impose their will. MacGillivray, for instance, suggests that 'Evans's Minoans are an example of how an archaeological discovery occurs first in the mind, born of the thinker's need to prove something of vital importance to himself. Finding proof in the dirt is the final stage in the process of wish-fulfillment' (MacGillivray 2000: 6). This provides a useful counter-narrative to the less critical biographies in which the excavator's luck results in them revealing the remains of past civilisations but it negates the materiality of Knossos itself. Whatever Evans was looking for, the Throne Room and the colourful frescoes his excavations uncovered in 1900 shaped his response to the site. They also immediately aroused public interest, just as Schliemann's discovery of the Shaft Graves and 'Mask of Agamemnon' at Mycenae did in 1876. Even though both excavators were adept promoters of their discoveries who aroused press interest by tying them to Greek mythology, their finds were undeniably impressive. Visitors still travel to see the sites of Knossos, Mycenae and Troy and the museums where these finds are displayed, showing that while excavators can act as promoters and even reconstructors of their sites and finds, their role as creators is always constrained to some extent by their discoveries. Recent cultural histories of these sites have broadened the focus, examining the intertwined histories of excavators, sites and the reception of these discoveries (Gere 2006; Mac Sweeney 2018; Whitley 2024).

Only a few Aegean prehistorians have been the subject of full-length biographies, often celebratory in tone. They give a skewed impression of the field even if some recent biographies have tried to recognise more marginalised figures. Harriet Boyd Hawes and Winifred Lamb were among the first women to lead excavations in the Aegean (Allsebrook 1992; Gill 2018). Three men who excavated in Crete have also been the subject of biographies: Duncan Mackenzie (Momigliano 1999), Richard Seager (Becker and Betancourt 1997) and John Pendlebury (Grundon 2007). Autobiographies and memoirs also exist, including that of David Hogarth, director of the British School at Athens and collaborator with Arthur Evans at Knossos (Hogarth 1910). These are often useful for establishing excavators' opinions and motivations even if some read uncomfortably today. Such works, and the numerous shorter papers about archaeologists' lives, are important building blocks of disciplinary history. There is an important distinction, however, between works which establish individual archaeologists as 'pioneers' or 'heroes' and those which seek to understand them within their historical and intellectual context. There is increasing interest in 'life-writing' in archaeology in general for this reason (Lewis and Moshenska 2023). Christos Tsountas, for instance, is a significant figure not just because of his important excavations at Mycenae, Vapheio, Dimini and Sesklo but because he helped to incorporate the Mycenaeans within the Greek national identity (Andreou 2005; Voutsaki 2017). Arthur Evans performed a similar role for Cretan identity by establishing the Minoans as the first European civilisation (Hamilakis and Momigliano 2006; Galanakis 2014). But in order to understand these contributions fully, it is necessary to turn away from individuals to look at these wider historical and intellectual frameworks.

The same can be said for a closely related genre, that of institutional history. Anniversaries are often marked by publications, celebrating the work of the Archaeological Society at Athens (Petrakos 1987) or the Foreign Schools of archaeology (Waterhouse 1986; Étienne 1996; Korka 2007). Minoan archaeology was featured prominently in books marking the centenary of excavations on Crete, although the centenary year depended on national perspective (La Rosa and Rizzo 1985; Huxley 2000; Muhly 2000). These books have been characterised as 'nationalistic and self-congratulatory' (Hamilakis and Momigliano 2006: 26), with the histories of Foreign Schools similarly as 'ancestor worship' (Hamilakis 2007: 48). Problems of tone aside, these publications often provide a useful summary of archaeological work by an institution or a group of scholars which is otherwise distributed across numerous site reports and monographs. As with biographies of individuals, what can be lacking is a wider historical and intellectual framework within which to understand these histories.

3 Intellectual Context

A deeper problem with the biographical approach is that the figure of the archaeologist is a modern creation, the product of the emergence of the scientific discipline of archaeology in the nineteenth century. Archaeology consisted, in an abstract sense, of a structured body of knowledge about the past. This knowledge was brought into being through the meetings of learned societies, publications in scientific journals and the display of finds in a systematic way. Excavation became a characteristic method of archaeology as a formalised way for extracting artefacts out of the ground. Press reports and popular books helped establish archaeologists as public figures whose discoveries were the subject of widespread interest. Heinrich Schliemann, Sir Arthur Evans and Christos Tsountas came to epitomise prehistoric Aegean archaeology but they did not create the institutions which they adeptly used to promote their discoveries.

The intellectual context of Aegean Prehistory in the nineteenth and early part of the twentieth century can be split into two related fields of inquiry. Both lie at the intersection of text and the newly emerging science of archaeology. The first field focussed on the question of origins, or 'Who were the Greeks?'. The study of the evolutionary origins of mankind, with its attendant theories of race and population movements, was aligned with the theories of ancient authors about the earliest inhabitants of Greece and Asia Minor. Scientific practices of classification and typology, whether of pottery, skulls or languages, were used to elucidate this question. The second is the 'Homeric Question', actually a set of questions about the origins of the *Iliad* and the *Odyssey*, but particularly relevant to archaeologists was the question of the historicity of the Trojan War and related myths. This was increasingly addressed through the practice of fieldwork and excavation. These questions and practices were intertwined in the development of Aegean Prehistory.

Archaeologists weren't the first people to uncover ancient graves and identify their inhabitants by the style of their grave goods. The historian Thucydides[1] has been credited with archaeological reasoning by identifying the occupants of graves in Delos as Carian because of their characteristic weapons (Cook 1955). According to Thucydides the colonisers of the Aegean islands were Phoenicians and Carians and so the grave goods confirmed the tradition. Herodotus provides a more detailed account of the tradition: the Carians, or Leleges, inhabited the islands at the time of King Minos before they were displaced by the Dorians and Ionians.[2] He goes on to say that the Carians of his day, that is the occupants of Caria in Anatolia, regarded themselves as autochthonous, that is the original inhabitants of the land. Elsewhere he names the Pelasgians as the original inhabitants of Greece.[3]

---

[1] Thucydides, *The Peloponnesian War* 1.8.1. [2] Herodotus, *Histories* 1.171.
[3] Herodotus, *Histories* 1.56.2.

During the eighteenth and nineteenth century a revival of interest in the history of the Greeks resulted in a large body of scholarship on ancient Greek history, language and art. In Germany this came to be defined as *Altertumswissenschaft*, the science of antiquity. One of the key eighteenth-century figures was Johann Joachim Winckelmann who was able to isolate and chart the stylistic development of Greek art through his careful studies of ancient sculpture in Rome. In Britain the Society of the Dilettanti, founded 1734, began to sponsor the study and publication of ancient sculpture and architecture in the Aegean. Alongside art history, the study of philology also grew in this period in the wake of the recognition that Greek, Latin and Sanskrit, as well as most European languages, were all descendants of a common 'Indo-European' ancestor. This helped foster an interest in the movements of ancient peoples in order to explain the distribution of Indo-European languages which stimulated ancient historians to analyse ancient authors' accounts of Greek origins. Karl Müller, for instance, embarked on a history of Greek peoples but only completed volumes on the Minyans, the original inhabitants of Orchomenos in Boeotia, and the Dorians (Müller 1820, 1824). His contemporary at the University of Göttingen, Karl Hoeck, wrote a history of Crete which went back to the time of Minos and before; he used the term 'minoisch', Minoan, to describe this early period (Hoeck 1823–29; Karadimas and Momigliano 2004; Karadimas 2015: 5–7). George Grote's twelve-volume *History of Greece* began with a description of 'Legendary Greece', but he suggested that 'real history of Greece' only began in 776 BCE (Grote 1846: vii). It was only when Ernst Curtius, who had written his own history of Greece, came to excavate at Olympia in 1875 that archaeology as a discipline became a significant component of *Altertumswissenschaft* (Morris 1994: 25).

Another key figure of *Altertumswissenschaft* was Friedrich August Wolf, whose 1795 book *Prolegomena ad Homerum* opened up the Homeric Question. Wolf (1795) applied philological methods to the *Iliad* and the *Odyssey* to question their authorship. The previous decades had seen a growth of interest in the setting of the *Iliad*. A French expedition had mapped the Troad, the region on the north east coast of the Aegean which had been traditionally associated with Troy and whose topography had been described by Homer. One of its members, Jean Baptiste Lechevalier (1799), put forward the theory that a mountainous site called Bournabashi was the site of Homeric Troy. This identification was partly inspired by the Greek geographer Strabo, who argued that Homeric Troy was in a different place from later Greek and Roman Troy (Ilion/Ilium). The latter site, at Hissarlik, had been identified by another member of the French team, Franz Kauffer. This identification was confirmed by a numismatist, Edward Clarke, who had acquired coins from this site (Cook

1973: 46–8, 94). These scholars helped to establish discussions of the topography of Troy as another aspect of the Homeric Question. Subsequent travellers generally accepted Bournabashi as Homeric Troy, including William Gell, whose description and watercolour sketches of the area were published in *The Topography of Troy* (Gell 1804).

Mycenae also attracted interest in the same period, although, like Tiryns, its remains had never entirely disappeared. The problem became one of fitting it into the sequence of Greek art. William Gell (1810) also visited Mycenae and his resulting sketch of the Lion Gate was published in a Society of the Dilettanti publication, *Specimens Of Antient Sculpture* (Figure 2). It was described by Richard Payne Knight in the accompanying text: 'The most antient monument of Grecian sculpture now extant is unquestionably the broken piece of natural relief in the ancient portal to the gates of Mycenae, which is probably the same that belonged to the capital of Agamemnon, and may therefore be at least as old as the age of Daedalus' (Payne Knight 1809: xvii). This shows an attempt to extend Winckelmann's sequence of Greek art back beyond the Archaic period. The Lion Gate was illustrated alongside a Bronze Age sealstone acquired by Gell with similar iconography, successfully extending a stylistic typology from architecture to smaller prehistoric antiquities (Krzyszkowska 2005: 311–2).

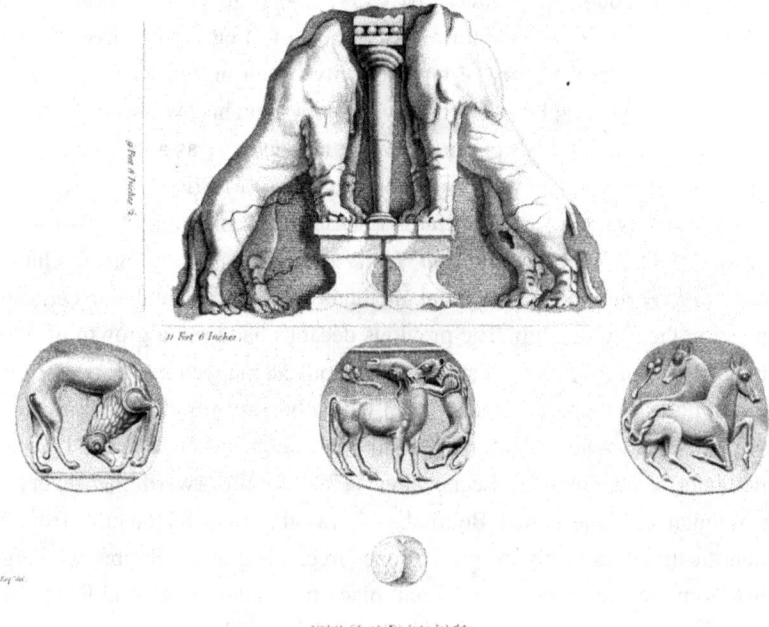

Figure 2 Drawing of Lion Gate and sealstone by William Gell (Payne Knight 1809: lxxxi).

Gell was joined on this trip by Edward Dodwell whose own drawings of Mycenae were later published in *Views and Descriptions of Cyclopian, or Pelasgic Remains in Greece and Italy* (Dodwell 1834). Cyclopian (or Cyclopean) was the term used by the ancient geographer Pausanias to describe the architecture of Mycenae and Tiryns, with walls made from large blocks which looked like they had been built by giants. For Dodwell and others this became a marker of Pelasgians, the original inhabitants of this area.

The middle of the nineteenth century is generally seen as the emergence of the discipline or science of archaeology (Trigger 1989: 73; Schnapp 1996: 275–315). An important debate about the 'Antiquity of Man' revolved around the explanation of the remains of extinct animals with early stone tools in stratified deposits. Among the protagonists were Sir John Evans, father of Arthur Evans, who in 1859 helped investigate one instance in the Somme valley for the Royal Society of London. This helped overturn the short 6000-year chronology for humanity derived from the Bible and instead necessitated a much longer chronology derived from the newly developed science of geology. This chronological extension in turn allowed the recognition that humans had evolved from 'lower' life forms rather than being creations of God. The mechanism for this was put forward by Charles Darwin in his 1859 book *The Origin of Species*, and was later extended to the humans in *The Descent of Man* (1871). This evolutionism and long chronology complemented the idea of the technological progress of humanity. A Danish museum curator, Christian Thomsen, classified his collection into successive Stone, Bronze and Iron Ages (Schnapp 1996: 299–301). Later on the Stone Age was divided by Sir John Lubbock (1865) into an earlier Palaeolithic phase and a later Neolithic phase. Lubbock also introduced a moral dimension that was often implicit in nineteenth-century scholarship: that technological progress followed the path from savagery to civilisation. Lubbock's book *Pre-historic Times* popularised the term 'prehistory', although it goes back to 1851 (Daniel 1950: 76).

The emergence of prehistoric archaeology in the Aegean is more complicated because there was already a mytho-historical framework in use which provided a chronological sequence back into what could now be called the Bronze Age. The three-age system did offer a new means to categorise stone tools, which had long been collected locally but were now starting to come into the hands of scholars engaged in this international dialogue. Prominent among these was George Finlay, who amassed a large collection of stone tools, even sending some to Sir John Evans. He produced a pamphlet which identified them as Neolithic and compared them to the prehistoric finds emerging from the Swiss lakes, which were capturing public attention (Finlay 1869). The pamphlet was only published in Greek and had limited impact, although Tsountas developed Finlay's ideas about lake dwellers as the ancestors of the Mycenaeans (Tsountas and Manatt 1897: 329–30; Runnels 2008). Albert Dumont also travelled around Greece to catalogue Neolithic stone tools, and even mentions a Palaeolithic hand axe (Dumont 1867a: 18; 1867b). Palaeolithic sites were not recognised in Greece until the 1920s (Kourtessi-Philippakis 2006).

The three-age system emerged as a means to classify artefacts in museums, with stratified excavation subsequently providing an important test of its validity. Although the principles of stratigraphic excavation were well established by the time Schliemann started to excavate Troy in 1870, he instead chose to dig a trench straight to the bottom of the mound of Hissarlik in search of the Homeric levels. In this way he was answering the Homeric Question as articulated in the early nineteenth century. It was only subsequently that Schliemann's assistant, Wilhelm Dörpfeld, who had excavated at Olympia, defined the strata of Hissarlik accurately (Dörpfeld 1902). Since the other Bronze Age sites excavated in the nineteenth century were predominately tombs, they did not help to refine Aegean Bronze Age stratigraphy. Instead they produced a wealth of material that art historians could classify, using methods which went back to Winckelmann. One of the most important examples of this approach was Adolf Furtwängler and Georg Loeschcke's (1879, 1886) illustrated corpora of Mycenaean pottery (Figure 3). These publications, *Mycenaean Pottery* and *Mycenaean Vases*, also helped to establish Mycenae as the type site for this

Figure 3 Drawings of pottery vessels from Ialysos (Furtwängler and Loeschke 1886: pl. II).

style of pottery and hence the society in general. Bronze Age sealstones, initially referred to as 'island gems', were also included and later became subjects of separate corpora and typologies (Furtwängler 1900). These Mycenaean finds were also rapidly incorporated within discussions about the history of Greek art and ancient art more generally (Milchhöfer 1883; Dumont and Chaplain 1888; Perrot and Chipiez 1894a, 1894b). It was only in the twentieth century that the potential of mounds for revealing complex stratification was realised, with Knossos, Korakou and the tumuli of Thessaly and Macedonia all contributing to the delineation of different phases of the Neolithic and Bronze Age.

From the start 'Mycenaean' was used to describe a culture or civilisation as well as a style of art (Furtwängler and Loeschcke 1879: 1; Tsountas 1893; Perrot and Chipiez 1894b: 468), but the problem became how to map this on to the traditional ethnic groups of Greece. Christos Tsountas turned to Homeric ethnonyms: the people buried in the Shaft Graves were Danaans and the tholos-tomb builders were Achaeans. Schliemann came to see the Mycenaeans as Phoenician colonists (Schliemann 1885: 28); for William Ridgeway (1901: 277) they were synonymous with the Pelasgians. The Aegean islanders were often seen as Carians and Leleges after Thucydides (Tsountas and Manatt 1897: 258). Despite this mix of peoples Tsountas and others were keen to see the Mycenaeans as forerunners of the later Greeks. The concept of a Greek spirit or genius emerged to demonstrate this continuity (Perrot and Chipiez 1894a: 7; Voutsaki 2002). This was particularly important for Tsountas as he sought to extend the history of the Greeks backwards into prehistory, developing the work of historian Constantine Paparrigopoulos. This work had a nationalistic aim in demonstrating that the present-day people of Greece were the descendants and inheritors of earlier Hellenic cultures (Voutsaki 2017: 136–7).

Chronological debates were largely answered using Egyptian archaeology. In 1870 the British Museum acquired a scarab of Amenhotep III, found in association with Mycenaean pottery at Ialysos on Rhodes.[4] Charles Newton, keeper of Greek and Roman Antiquities at the Museum, who had taken an early interest in Mycenaean culture, pointed out its importance for dating to Heinrich Schliemann (Schliemann 1878: 65–6; Newton 1880: 294). Newton's dates for the Mycenaean period were too low, however, because he regarded the scarab as an heirloom (Fitton 1995: 32). The chronology was refined by Sir Flinders Petrie, who discovered Mycenaean pottery in Egypt in the 1890s and also visited Greece to examine Egyptian finds from Mycenaean sites (Petrie 1890, 1891; Phillips 2006). The Egyptian dates aligned well with the

---

[4] British Museum GR 1870,1008.130.

traditional Greek chronology derived from ancient authors, with the Trojan War ending in 1184 BCE. As a result they were not entirely disruptive to earlier schemes based on this tradition: both William Gell and William Leake, for instance, were broadly correct in dating Tiryns and Mycenae to the fourteenth century BCE (Gell 1810: 29, 54; Leake 1830: 354–5). For others the terms 'heroic' or 'pre-Homeric' vaguely referred to the time of the Trojan War. In general the Egyptian dates helped to extend the time depth of the Mycenaean period. Petrie also recognised 'Aegean' pottery at Gurob, which was subsequently recognised by John Myres as being identical to pottery he saw in Heraklion in 1893. This 'Kamares' pottery had been found by a shepherd in the Kamares Cave in southern Crete (Brown 1986). As a result the chronology of Bronze Age Crete was established in outline even before Evans began excavating at Knossos.

The excavation of Knossos resulted in a synthesis between European prehistory and Mycenaean archaeology. Although Arthur Evans and Duncan Mackenzie initially referred to pottery as 'Mycenaean' and 'Kamares', five years later Evans published his tripartite scheme which classified Minoan pottery into Early, Middle and Late periods, each subdivided into three phases (Evans 1906a) (Figure 4). This marked the imposition of evolutionism since there was an explicit recognition that these periods and their subdivisions traced the rise, maturity and decay of the Minoan civilisation (Evans 1921: 25; McNeal 1973; Hamilakis 2002). The scheme was extended to the mainland following the excavations of Carl Blegen at the mound of Korakou (Wace and Blegen 1918; McNeal 1975). He and Alan Wace eschewed the cultural labels 'Minyan' and 'Mycenaean' and described the pottery as Early, Middle and Late Helladic instead, suggesting 'Cycladic' as the equivalent term for the islands. Stratified Cycladic pottery had been excavated at Phylakopi on Melos in 1896–9 and one of the excavators, Duncan Mackenzie, had established synchronisms with Minoan pottery from Knossos (Mackenzie 1904). The tripartite scheme was subsequently applied to Macedonia by William Heurtley (1939) after his stratigraphic excavation of several mounds. Over time the pottery chronologies, particularly Minoan and Mycenaean pottery, were further subdivided as a result of Arne Furumark's (1941) typology of Mycenaean pottery. This used shape and decoration as the basis for assigning dates to vessels and is in the long tradition of typological study of Mycenaean pottery initiated by Furtwängler and Loeschcke.

With the excavation of Crete in the early twentieth century, particularly Palaikastro, the number of skulls available for study multiplied (Bosanquet *et al.* 1903: 274–5). This in turn allowed the application of craniometry to the Aegean Bronze Age, and with it the identification of racial categories. Although terms 'Aryan' and 'race' do occur frequently in nineteenth-century works they

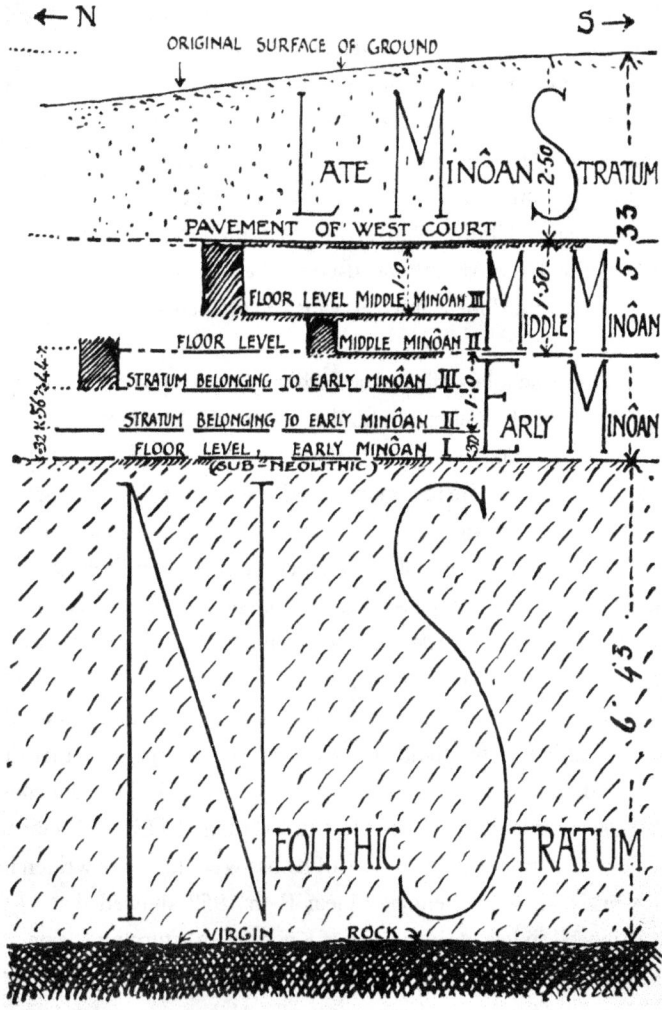

Figure 4 Drawing of section of West Court at Knossos (Evans 1921: fig. 4).

largely relate to ideas about language and culture. The theory of Aryan migrations was developed by Max Müller (1856), but he saw this in linguistic terms. For Schliemann, who corresponded with Müller, it was clear that the Trojans were Aryans, and Tsountas used this term to describe the Mycenaeans too (Schliemann 1875: 16; Tsountas and Manatt 1897: 314). Craniometry, however, changed the debate by distinguishing brachycephalic (broad-headed) Aryans from dolichocephalic (long-headed) non-Aryans. One of the protagonists was Charles Hawes, who suggested that the Minoans were long-headed, non-Aryan and members of the Mediterranean race (Hawes and Hawes 1911: 22–3, 147). The concept of the 'Mediterranean race' was put forward by Giuseppe Sergi

(1901b) as a counterbalance to the idea that a Germanic Aryan race came from northern Europe. Sergi himself studied skulls from Italian excavations on Crete of what were considered to be Mycenaean tombs, declaring their features to be 'peculiar to the Mediterranean race' (Sergi 1901a: 318). In this way discussions about linguistic origins became increasingly racialised in the early twentieth century, although some authors continued to use the term 'Aryan' primarily as a linguistic division (Childe 1926). Ultimately the theory equating a Nordic or Germanic race with the Aryans was used by the Nazi Party to justify genocide. This largely ended the debate about Aryans and racial origins in Greece after the Second World War.

Like many other scholars of his time Arthur Evans adopted these racial theories (Evans 1921: 7–9). He embraced the theory that the Minoans were non-Greek although Greek mythology helped to show the previous glories of the Minoan civilisation. Nevertheless he regarded the Minoans as the first European civilisation (Evans 1921: 1; Schoep 2018). For him the Shaft Grave finds showed that the Minoans had conquered mainland Greece, passing civilisation on to the Mycenaeans, who had in turn passed it on to Classical Greece. This added another chapter to the story of the Greeks told by Tsountas but complicated it by invoking an invasion rather than continuous progression from the Neolithic (Andreou 2005: 78–9). This idea of Minoan primacy led to a vigorous dispute with Alan Wace, whose dating of the tholos tombs at Mycenae suggested that they were instead local developments (Wace et al. 1923; Evans 1929; Galanakis 2015). Evans had also maintained until his death in 1941 that the Linear B tablets he had excavated in the final destruction levels of Knossos could not be written in Greek. Michael Ventris' decipherment of Linear B in 1952 showed that Mycenaean Greek was indeed in use at the palace of Knossos, overturning Evans' narrative and shifting the debate about the origin of the Greeks.

The nineteenth century had been an era of decipherments, with first Egyptian hieroglyphs and then the Middle Eastern cuneiform writing system understood. Writing was seen as a marker of civilisation, and Evans had gone to Crete in search of an early writing system, rapidly finding examples of two scripts, Cretan Hieroglyphic and Linear A. The third, Linear B, was found on clay tablets in the first year of excavation at Knossos but, despite his efforts, Evans was unable to decipher any of these scripts. Other scholars before Ventris, including Alice Kober and Emmett Bennett, had identified patterns in the Linear B tablets but were hampered by Evans' failure to publish them fully in his lifetime (Chadwick 1958; Fox 2013). In 1906, however, the discovery and subsequent decipherment of Hittite cuneiform tablets at the site of Boğazköy offered to shed light on the history of Mycenaean Greece. It was soon realised that the city 'Wilusa' mentioned in the tablets could be Homeric Ilios. Forrer (1924) was the first to suggest that the people called 'Ahhiyawa' mentioned in these texts could be Homer's Achaeans. The 'Ahhiyawa Question' continues to be debated between those who would equate this group with Mycenaean Greece and others who prefer a more restricted area such as Rhodes (Beckman *et al.* 2011: 1–6). The importance of this debate is that Achaean could be a contemporary term for a group of people rather than a later name retrospectively applied to an archaeological assemblage. In order to understand the political implications of the language spoken in Mycenaean Greece, it is necessary to turn from the Homeric Question to the 'Eastern Question'.

4 Political and Institutional History of Archaeology in the Aegean

From the late eighteenth century onwards the politics of the Aegean were dominated by what western European politicians and diplomats called the 'Eastern Question'. This centred on the gradual dissolution of the Ottoman Empire in response to local revolts and the question of what should happen to its former territories. The creation of a Greek kingdom in 1832 by the 'Great Powers' of the day, Britain, France and Russia, provided one answer, partly based on a desire to resurrect ancient Greece. The borders of Greece continued to expand until 1922 when the Ottoman Empire finally collapsed and Greek territorial ambitions in Anatolia ended with the burning of Smyrna. The Republic of Turkey came into being the following year. These political events helped to shape the emergence of archaeology in the Aegean by constraining, and sometimes favouring, the activities of travellers, and later archaeologists. Many of them were also collectors of antiquities, on behalf of themselves or institutions in their home countries. Travel, exporting antiquities and excavation were all dependent on the laws, conventions and political stability of particular territories in the Aegean, many of which shifted from Ottoman to Greek control during the period in which Aegean Prehistory emerged. The following section provides an outline of the framework within which archaeology developed in the Ottoman Empire and the way in which this changed as areas of the Aegean became part of Greece.

4.1 Ottoman Empire and Turkey

Nine years after the Ottoman conquest of Constantinople (Istanbul) in 1453, Sultan Mehmet II is said to have visited Troy and declared that he had avenged the Trojans (Rose 2013: 282–3). In doing so he was claiming his role in an imagined conflict between East and West that went back to the Trojan War. He was not the first historical figure to have visited Troy for this reason: Julius Caesar and Alexander the Great were among his predecessors. Unlike them, it is not clear whether he visited the Greek and Roman city of Ilium at Hissarlik, where prehistoric Troy was subsequently excavated in the nineteenth century. But his visit does show how archaeological sites, history and politics can become entangled in the Aegean. Between 1463 and 1718 the Ottoman Empire expanded across the Aegean as a result of a series of wars with Venice, the former colonial power in the region. Only the Ionian islands remained under Venetian control. Once these wars had concluded, the places described by Homer, and the cities of Classical Greece, became more accessible to travellers.

The search for, and removal of, classical antiquities from the Ottoman Empire to western Europe goes back to at least the seventeenth century. Since the administration of the Empire was centred on the court of the Sultan, permission to remove antiquities came in the form of a personal decree, or firman, from the Sultan or one of his representatives. It is not accidental that a number of westerners who held the post of ambassador to the Sublime Porte, as the Sultan's government was known, used their position to gain permission to export antiquities as part of their wider mission to enable trade. One of the first was Thomas Roe, who during his term as English ambassador to Constantinople from 1621 to 1628 helped to acquire antiquities for the Duke of Buckingham and Earl of Arundel. Arundel's collection, which consisted largely of Greek and Roman inscriptions and sculpture, did not contain prehistoric material but was one of the first collections of antiquities in Britain (Vickers 2006).

Subsequent ambassadors to the Sublime Porte can be more closely associated with the development of Aegean Prehistory. Comte Choiseul-Gouffier served as French ambassador from 1784 to 1791. He was particularly interested in the antiquity of the region and employed a number of specialist cartographers and artists to record antiquities, as well as remove them when possible. His collection of antiquities is now in the Louvre. He also commissioned the first survey of the Troad, undertaken by Lechevalier and Kauffer. The second volume of his *Voyage Pittoresque de la Grèce*, published in 1809, included a map of the Troad with the two contending sites for Troy marked, Bournabashi (Ilium Vetus or Old Troy) and Hissarlik (Ilium Novum, or New Troy) (Choiseul-Gouffier 1809: pl. 19). One of his agents conducted the first recorded excavation in the region, in the so-called Tomb of Achilles. Like other features of the Troad this mound had been given Homeric associations but turned out to be classical in date (Allen 1999: 42).

Lord Elgin, British ambassador in Constantinople from 1798 to 1803, also used his position to acquire and export antiquities from across the Aegean. Like Choiseul-Gouffier before him he sent agents to remove sculptures from the Athenian Acropolis with the support of a now disputed firman. These, and sculptures from the Troad and mainland Greece, ended up in the British

Museum as a result of the sale of his collection to the nation in 1816. Among the sculptures he exported with the support of another firman were several Mycenaean sculptural slabs collected from the Treasury of Atreus at Mycenae. An early guide to the Elgin collection at the British Museum describes them as Cyclopean, suggesting that they go back to 'to the remotest period of which man has left distinct evidence of his existence' (Ellis 1833: 117), while a later curator noted that 'they may be authentic memorials of a dynasty only dimly remembered in the Homeric poems' (Smith 1892: 12). As a result of the diplomatic network which connected London and the Aegean, original prehistoric sculpture was the subject of learned speculation in London even before Schliemann's excavations at Mycenae.

Below the level of ambassador there was a network of consuls and vice-consuls who represented foreign governments in major cities and ports across the Empire. Their role was mainly to facilitate trade, and, particularly at the level of vice-consul, these roles were often filled by local businessmen. In return for representing foreign governments they received some level of diplomatic protection and could also profit from the connections they made with merchants. These figures also sometimes played a role in the acquisition of antiquities, particularly during the nineteenth century (Gunning 2009). Charles Newton was one example, whose career began at the British Museum before he became vice-consul in Mytilene and consul on Rhodes in the 1850s. The British ambassador at the time was Stratford Canning, who had lobbied Ottoman officials for permission to acquire sculptures for the British Museum from various parts of the Empire; his demands helped stimulate the foundation of an antiquities museum in Istanbul in 1846 (Özkaya 2022). Canning enabled Newton to undertake excavations, particularly at Halicarnassus, and then to arrange transfer of objects to the British Museum using the British Navy. Newton returned to the Museum as the keeper of the Department of Greece and Rome in 1861 but maintained his contacts with this area and acquired objects from, among others, the excavations of John Turtle Wood at Ephesus and his protégé Alfred Biliotti on Rhodes. Biliotti spent his career in the consular service but supplemented his income by excavating and selling antiquities (Barchard 2006). In 1868 he began excavating Mycenaean chamber tombs at Ialysos, whose contents were purchased by the British Museum.

The first Ottoman antiquities bylaw was passed in 1869 partly as a result of a process of modernisation known at the Tanzimat reforms and partly as a response to the extraction of antiquities from sites such as Ephesus (Eldem 2011). This law established an Imperial Museum in Istanbul (re-establishing the earlier antiquities museum), created a system of permissions for excavators and also prohibited the export of antiquities. This did not entirely prevent the export of antiquities because the Sultan was still able to override the law, and antiquities remained in private ownership. In 1874 a new, more liberal, antiquities law further loosened the rules on export but following a number of high-profile cases, including the removal of the hellenistic altar from Pergamon and Priam's Treasure from Troy, the law was changed again ten years later. The 1884 law brought antiquities into state ownership, with finds to go to the Imperial Museum, and made excavators define sites using maps when asking for permission to dig. Another law of 1906 expanded the definition of antiquities further to include Islamic archaeology for the first time. This law remained in force until 1973 (Shaw 2003; Bahrani et al. 2011).

The Imperial Museum was moved to a new purpose-built location in 1891, which remains the home of the Istanbul Archaeological Museum. The Imperial Museum adopted an active acquisitions policy, particularly under the leadership of Hamdi Bey, who undertook his own excavations in the Levant. He was succeeded as director by Makridi Bey, who excavated two prehistoric mounds in Ottoman Macedonia. The Museum was intended to be the repository for antiquities from across the Ottoman Empire instead of overseas museums. Sherds from Troy, however, were seen as less important and so the Imperial Museum allowed the export of these to Berlin in 1885 (Shaw 2003: 117). The presence of the Museum was to have a chilling effect on the archaeology of Crete while it remained under Ottoman control. The excavations of Minos Kalokairinos at Knossos were rapidly shut down by the local authorities in 1879 because of a fear that major finds would be sent to Istanbul (MacGillivray 2000: 89).

Under the new regime of Mustafa Kemal Atatürk, the centre of government was moved to Ankara and an archaeological museum was founded there in 1921. Ankara soon became the capital of the Republic of Turkey with Atatürk as its first president. A Hittite Museum was subsequently opened on a different site in 1945. Both museums were related to a policy to cultivate a national identity based on the previous inhabitants of Turkey, particularly the Hittites (Savino 2012). The Hittite capital, Hattusa, had been recognised at Boğazköy in the nineteenth century and was subsequently excavated by French and then German archaeologists. Makridi Bey was also involved in this excavation, signalling the priorities of Ottoman archaeologists in this period. In 1929 the Deutsches Archäologisches Institut (DAI) opened a department in Istanbul to co-ordinate its activities in Turkey. The following year saw the creation of l'Institut Français d'Archéologie, also in Istanbul. British and American research institutes were only established after the Second World War. This contrasts with a much longer tradition of Foreign Schools of archaeology in Greece.

4.2 Greece

The Greek War of Independence began in 1821, resulting in the foundation of the Kingdom of Greece in 1832. This initially encompassed the Peloponnese, Central Greece and a number of Aegean islands. Philhellenism, looking back to the glories of classical Greece, played an important role in the independence movement and also inspired its various foreign backers including Britain and France. For this reason Greek antiquities rapidly became significant totems for the revolutionaries and decrees on their protection were made as early as 1825. The focus was primarily on ancient Greek inscriptions and sculpture since prehistoric antiquities were little known at this point. At the Fourth National Assembly of 1829 a ban on the export of antiquities was passed and a national museum was founded at Aegina (Voudouri 2008, 2017). As part of the 1832 Treaty of Constantinople, which brought Greece into being, a Bavarian Prince, Otto, was installed on the throne. One of Otto's councillors, Georg Ludwig von Maurer, drafted the first Greek antiquities law which was passed in 1834 (Voudouri 2017: 78). This brought the Antiquities Service, which had been formed the previous year, under the leadership of the newly established Ephor General of Antiquities. The first Ephor was Ludwig Ross, a German classicist, who travelled around Greece and took an interest in a variety of prehistoric sites and objects (Petrakos 2009).

The foundation of the Archaeological Society of Athens in 1837 was intended to complement the Antiquities Service. Independent of the state and funded through private subscriptions, many of its members were Greek, although foreign scholars were also admitted. Nevertheless it acted like a state body (Voudouri 2017: 81). The Archaeological Society began to conduct excavations in Athens before expanding to other parts of Greece over the course of the nineteenth century. Its primary concern was with classical sites and antiquities although its members did engage in prehistoric excavations too. It also established important fora for the publication of archaeological research, the *Proceedings of the Archaeological Society* (Πρακτικά της εν Αθήναις Αρχαιολογικής Εταιρείας) and its *Archaeological Journal* (Αρχαιολογική Εφημερίς), which have been published continuously since 1837 (Petrakos 1987: 189–93).

The National Museum was moved from Aegina to the new Greek capital, Athens, in 1834. It continued to accumulate antiquities, many from the excavations of the Archaeological Society. Objects were displayed in various buildings around Athens, principally the Hephaisteion, until a new purpose-built neoclassical museum opened in 1889. A new law was passed in 1893 defining the purpose of the National Archaeological Museum as for the study and teaching of archaeology as well as the diffusion of archaeological knowledge rather than simply safeguarding objects. The law also defined departments including a prehistoric section (Avgouli 1994: 247, 254; Gazi 2017: 99). By this time prehistoric finds from Mycenae, Vapheio and the Cycladic islands were available for display. The Museum's arrangement was overseen by the Ephor, Panagiotis Kavvadias, assisted by Christos Tsountas and Valerios Stais. Stais became curator of vases and then director, and also wrote the first catalogue of Mycenaean antiquities (Kokkou 1977: 248–9; Petrochilos 1992: 20). All were archaeologists who had excavated prehistoric sites. As a result of the timing and personnel of the new National Archaeological Museum, Greek prehistory rapidly became a prominent part of the national collection. The first regional museum was opened at Sparta in 1874, with over thirty others founded in a burst at the start of the twentieth century (Gazi 2008, 2017: 100). These were largely funded by the Archaeological Society.

The institutionalisation of archaeology in Greece continued in the nineteenth century with the establishment of five Foreign Schools, representing France (1846), Germany (1874), the United States (1881), Great Britain (1886) and Austria-Hungary (1898) (Korka 2007). Although there were differences in organisation and funding, their main role was to facilitate the research of their members in Greece. The French School at Athens was founded by royal decree and was government-funded from the start. Similarly the German and Austrian schools were departments of state-funded central archaeological institutes. The American School of Classical Studies at Athens has always been a private body funded through donations from American universities and individuals. The British School at Athens began with private funding but soon came to receive supplementary funding from the British government (Macmillan 1911). The Italian School at Athens was founded in 1909 and the Swedish Archaeological School in 1948. Archaeologists from these nations had been active before this time, although the Italians had mainly worked on Crete and Swedish archaeologist had relied on permits acquired through the German or French Schools. It was this role of the Schools in regulating the work of foreign archaeologists that became particularly important to the organisation of archaeology in Greece. There are now nineteen Foreign Schools in operation.

From their inception the Foreign Schools negotiated with the Greek authorities for the rights to excavate sites, and sometimes to export finds. Their activity, initially at least, has often been described as colonial (Morris 1994: 25): although Greece was an independent state, it had been brought into being by some of the same powers, who continued to pursue an active foreign policy in the Eastern Mediterranean. The Foreign Schools also had considerable financial resources, compared to a poorly funded and overstretched Archaeological Service

(Hamilakis 2007: 102–3). As a result they could afford to invest significant sums in excavating prominent Greek sites on a large scale. The founding of the German Archaeological Institute in Athens was closely linked with the flagship excavation at Olympia. The French School initiated significant projects at Delos and Delphi. The American School developed an association with Corinth which continues to this day. The British School, despite early forays into classical Greek architecture at Kynosarges in Athens and Megalopolis, came to focus more on prehistoric sites (Macmillian 1911: x–xi; Whitley 2007: 65). One of its first significant excavations was at Phylakopi on Melos, where a large Bronze Age settlement was uncovered. Initially at least there was competition between the Schools to excavate antiquities that could be exported to museums in their home countries. Excavations also brought prestige, particularly given the idea that all civilised countries shared in classical Greek heritage.

The Foreign Schools soon established their own series of journals and monographs. These allowed excavators to disseminate their finds in their own language. The first to appear in 1876 was the *Mitteilungen des Deutschen Archäologischen Instituts, Athenische Abteilung*, followed by the *Bulletin de Correspondance Hellénique* in 1887 and the *Annual of the British School at Athens* in 1886. The American School only started to publish *Hesperia* in 1932 but this was preceded by the *American Journal of Archaeology*. This was established in 1885 as the journal of the American Institute of Archaeology, founded six years before, and from the start included news from excavations in the Eastern Mediterranean and further afield. Similarly the *Journal of Hellenic Studies* started to publish an annual report, 'Archaeology in Greece', in 1887 which covered both excavations and museums. In 1889 the German Archaeological Institute took over the publication of *Der Archäologische Anzeiger*, which provided a digest of the work of its various departments including Athens, but this report started to include other excavations too. These publications helped to disseminate information about archaeological research, including those included in the Greek-language reports of the Archaeological Society. By comparing various excavations these publications also helped to formalise the practice of archaeology and create a structure within which archaeological research could take place. Conversely excavations which were not published in this way became less significant.

In 1899 a new law was passed which sought to stem the trade in antiquities by declaring them all state property. The previous law of 1834 had attempted to regulate excavations on private land but did little in practice to prevent people from buying and selling the resulting finds, allowing a flourishing antiquities market to develop (Galanakis 2011: 186–92). One of the most significant and notorious Bronze Age finds to appear on the market was the 'Aegina Treasure', which was purchased by the British Museum in 1891 (Evans 1893). Although it was said to come from Aegina, its origins remain unclear (Fitton et al. 2009). Overseas museums could still acquire material after 1899 since there was a provision in the new law which allowed for the export of objects declared 'useless' or 'redundant'. This left open the possibility for Foreign Schools to export material from their excavations, or other exchanges of objects, and sherd material was exported after this date (Frödin and Persson 1938: 12; Stefani and Shapland forthcoming). This became more difficult as a result of a further law of 1932 which placed further restrictions on the export of excavated material (Voudouri 2008: 127–9). Even though the legal framework restricted the activities of the archaeologists of the Foreign Schools, overseas museums continued to acquire objects from Greece after 1899. Cycladic material in particular has long been sought after by museums in Europe and America (Gill and Chippindale 1993: 610; Galanakis 2013). Objects acquired in this way provide some of the best evidence for the continuation of undocumented excavations and the activities of antiquities dealers.

The territory of Greece grew several times over the course of the nineteenth and twentieth century (Beaton 2019). Thessaly moved from Ottoman to Greek control in 1881. The border shifted north again when Macedonia and Epirus became part of Greece following the Balkan Wars of 1912 and 1913, which marked the start of a period of turmoil in Greece. The First World War, which followed on from events in Sarajevo in 1914, can be seen as a continuation of the Balkan Wars. Greece remained neutral until 1917, partly because the King was aligned with the Central Powers and Prime Minister Venizelos sided with the Allies. This developed into the National Schism, with rival governments in Athens and Thessaloniki. Foreign archaeologists became involved in espionage, with Alan Wace turning the British School at Athens into a centre for military intelligence. Other archaeologists in uniform took the opportunity to excavate in the Aegean (Gill 2011a). Archaeologists serving in the Allied Army of the Orient in Macedonia were often involved in both activities (Shapland and Stefani 2017). Archaeological finds made by soldiers were brought to Thessaloniki and stored in separate British and French collections. Following the end of the War many of these finds were removed to the British Museum and the Louvre with the permission of the Greek government. These generous donations came at a time when Venizelos needed the support of the Allies for his territorial aspirations in Anatolia (Clogg 2017; Stefani and Shapland forthcoming). The *Megali Idea* sought to bring Constantinople and other areas of Asia Minor with Greek-speakers into a 'Greater Greece'. This attempted expansion came to an end with the expulsion of Greek forces and burning of Smyrna in what became known in Greece as the

'Catastrophe' of 1922. The subsequent 'exchange of populations' resulted in a refugee crisis in both Athens and northern Greece which further challenged the state's resources and institutions after a decade of war.

The Second World War resulted in the Axis occupation of Greece by Italian, German and Bulgarian troops. Members of the Greek Archaeological Service remained in post and tried to protect archaeological sites, although episodes of looting occurred. As in the First World War in Macedonia, the digging of military installations also disturbed archaeological sites. Crete was particularly affected because of its strategic importance (Driessen 2024). Many museum collections were hidden or buried to prevent damage and theft. The German army operated a parallel '*Kunstschutz*', or 'art protection' programme and the German Archaeological Institute in Athens was also given a formal role in managing archaeological research (Matz 1951). The Civil War that immediately followed the Second World War in Greece continued until 1949, meaning that little archaeological activity happened again until the 1950s.

5 History of Archaeological Research in the Aegean

To some extent the history of excavation in each part of the Aegean is shaped by local circumstances, both geographical and historical. As has been suggested in Section 4, the different institutional and legal frameworks shaped archaeological research, either by constraining the activities of archaeologists or by providing opportunities. Periods of political instability also hampered archaeological activities, as on Crete, although in Macedonia the First World War provided opportunities for foreign archaeologists drafted into the Army of the Orient. Geography too played a role. The rocky citadels of Mycenae and Tiryns have always remained visible, whereas the mounds on the plains of Thessaly, Macedonia and Troy needed to be excavated to reveal the prehistoric levels.

Nevertheless, patterns are apparent. In most regions there was a period of survey, as travellers explored the landscape, initially trying to find sites mentioned in ancient texts. From the end of the eighteenth century, modern surveying techniques allowed detailed maps to be produced on which ancient remains were located. Many of these were linked to military activity, such as the French Morea Expedition, which mapped and described the Peloponnese and some of the islands, or the voyages of Captain Thomas Spratt to survey the Troad or Crete on behalf of the British Navy. Most foreign archaeologists, often with one of these maps in hand, conducted some sort of survey of their chosen area before they began to excavate. In almost every case, however, the popular narrative of discovery is false: archaeological sites were known locally and had frequently been excavated on a small scale by the local inhabitants too. Local collections, such as that of the Calvert family at

Çanakkale, Dimitrios Prasinos on Amorgos and Minos Kalokairinos in Heraklion provided an indication of what would be found at a given site.

During the nineteenth century, as archaeological authorities and local museums were founded, the state came to assume the role of collector, with state officials acting as intermediaries who ensured that finds were recorded. State officials, particularly the Greek Ephors, also performed the role of excavators but were often reliant on the resources of the Archaeological Society or Foreign Schools. They were also always in competition with the market, legal or otherwise, partly fuelled by the competition between western European and American museums to increase their collections. This ensured that many archaeological objects were excavated clandestinely or without record. It is difficult, however, to distinguish archaeological excavation from looting. Until the end of the nineteenth century it was legal for landowners in Greece and the Ottoman Empire to dig up antiquities on their land and sell them. Sometimes archaeologists commissioned locals to carry on their excavations, the only difference being that they made some sort of record. Over time excavation techniques and recording became increasingly formalised and publications more detailed, but standards of publication differed widely. The following provides a history of archaeological research by region, grouped according to political history. Ultimately, however, a history of archaeology is a history of archaeological publications, which translated monuments, excavations and objects into words and images.

5.1 Troad

Western travellers had been visiting the Troad in search of Troy since at least the sixteenth century. Pierre Belon, like many after him, visited the impressive hellenistic remains at Alexandria Troas and thought they were Troy (Belon 1555: 80–2; Cook 1973: 16). Belon was a naturalist who travelled around the Eastern Mediterranean and recorded plants and animals as well as archaeological sites. Jacob Spon and Charles Wheler visited Ilium in 1675, also collecting plant specimens and antiquities (Spon and Wheler 1678: 197–201). Robert Wood, a member of the Society of Dilettanti, visited Bournabashi in 1750 and published a book about Homer which contained his observations (Wood 1775). Hence even the research of Lechevalier instigated by Choiseul-Gouffier was in a long tradition of going in search of Homeric Troy (Lechevalier 1799; Choiseul-Gouffier 1809). The maps produced by Kauffer for Choiseul-Gouffier and by Captain Spratt, for the British Navy in 1839, provided scholars with more detailed information about topography.

Although many scholars followed Lechevalier's identification of Bournabashi, Charles Maclaren (1822, 1863) was one of the first to suggest that Hissarlik was

Homeric Troy. He finally visited Troy in 1847 and like many travellers at that time sought consular assistance at Çanakkale in the Dardanelles. The position of British vice-consul was held by members of the Calvert family, who had also established landholdings in the Troad. They took visitors on tours of the archaeological remains and also maintained a collection of antiquities found on their land, as the Ottoman law of this time allowed. Frank Calvert started excavating in 1853, perhaps stimulated by Maclaren's visit, although he dug at various places around the Troad before starting at Hissarlik (Ilium) (Allen 1999: 74). Another visitor who had encouraged his archaeological interests was Charles Newton, while he was consul at Rhodes (Newton 1865: 125). In 1863 Calvert wrote to him asking the British Museum to fund the dig at Hissarlik in return for the finds, but was turned down. Although Calvert continued digging in 1865, he was unable to continue his excavations for financial reasons. He only seems to have uncovered Greek and Roman remains but was convinced that he had found Homeric Troy. By his own account he shared this theory with Heinrich Schliemann when he visited in 1868 and called in to see the Calvert collection.

There is now little doubt that Schliemann's claim to have independently come to the conclusion that Hissarlik was Troy is false, as a forensic analysis of his diaries has shown (Traill 1995: 55–7; Allen 1999: 7). It is also doubtful that Schliemann's childhood dream was to excavate Troy since there is no evidence for any interest in Troy before 1868. By this time Schliemann had amassed a fortune from business and moved to Paris. His publications of his travels, first around Asia, and then around the Aegean, seem to have been an attempt to gain literary and academic prestige (Schliemann 1869). By this time there were already archaeological celebrities such as Paul-Émile Botta, whose finds from Assyria were displayed at the Louvre. Instead of acting as a wealthy backer to Frank Calvert, Schliemann decided to take over his excavations.

Schliemann excavated at Hissarlik between 1870 and 1873. The first season was cut short because he had started digging in the half of the mound that didn't belong to Calvert and was forced by the proprietors to stop. He had also failed to gain the necessary permissions under the newly passed archaeological law. Even so, he announced his discovery of Priam's Palace in a German newspaper, alerting Turkish officials to his excavation (Allen 1999: 131). From then on they took a close interest in his activities, and an overseer was appointed for his 1871 excavation under the terms of the firman that was eventually granted. He employed around 80 workers at first, increasing to 180 in later seasons, who enabled him to dig a trench down to the bottom of the 14 m high mound (Figure 5). His reasoning was that Priam's city was at the lowest level because it had only been founded two generations earlier by Priam's grandfather, Ilus. He subsequently recognised a new candidate for Priam's Palace at the bottom of the mound, and a nearby ramp which he named the 'Scaean

Figure 5 Photograph of the 'Schliemann Trench' through Hissarlik (Schliemann 1874: pl. 111).

Gate' after a toponym described in the *Iliad*. What distinguished Schliemann's approach from earlier attempts to discover Homeric Troy was the resources at his disposal, which allowed him to conduct large-scale excavations. His method of trying to match physical remains with descriptions from the *Iliad* was no different from previous scholars. Nor was he the first to use excavation as a method to explore Homeric sites: Calvert had dug at Hissarlik before him, and there had been other published excavations around the Plain of Troy.

One of Schliemann's contributions to Aegean Prehistory was his vigorous publication and promotion of his discoveries. This is exemplified by a find made in the 1873 season, which Schliemann dubbed 'Priam's Treasure'. This was a hoard of precious objects, including gold jewellery and silver vessels, as well as bronze tools and polished stone axes.[5] The finds were impressive in themselves but Schliemann's actions made them famous across the world. He rapidly smuggled them out of the Ottoman Empire to Athens to avoid having to cede some of the objects to the local authorities. He then published an account of his find in the *Augsburg Allgemeine Zeitung*, which was taken up by newspapers around the world (Traill 1995: 123). Photographs of the Treasure and other finds

---

[5] Now mostly in the Pushkin Museum in Moscow, the Hermitage in St Petersburg and a few pieces in the Museum für Vor- und Frühgeschichte in Berlin (Easton 1994).

were published the next year in his *Atlas trojanischer Alterthümer*, which was an early attempt to publish photographs of archaeological discoveries (Schliemann 1874). A popular account, *Troy and Its Remains*, appeared the next year and romanticised the story of their discovery, falsely claiming that his wife Sophia was there holding her shawl to gather the finds (Schliemann 1875: 323–4; Fitton 1995: 69). In 1877 Schliemann brought his Trojan finds to exhibit them in London, alongside some of his photographs (Baker 2019). The *Illustrated London News* covered his exhibition and a paper he gave at the Society of Antiquaries of London (Figure 6). Although many doubted whether

Figure 6 'Dr Schliemann giving an account of his discoveries at Mycenae before the Society of Antiquaries at Burlington House'. *Illustrated London News* 31 March 1877, p. 13.

these finds related directly to Priam, most agreed that they were prehistoric. Schliemann had used the mass media of the day to bring a selection of Bronze Age objects to the attention of a much wider audience than ever before.

For modern readers one of the most curious features of Schliemann's first publications about Troy is the amount of space he devoted to illustrating clay spindle-whorls. He suggested that incised symbols on some of them, particularly swastikas, provided evidence that the Trojans were Aryan (Schliemann 1875: 16). Some of the other marks he regarded as writing and published them in the hope that someone could decipher them. Archibald Sayce (1880) offered a nonsensical translation using the Cypriot syllabary. Subsequent excavations at Troy have failed to reveal any clay tablets analogous to the ones at Hattusa, and only one inscribed sealstone has been found to date (Rose 2013: 34–6). The other source of written evidence was Homer, and Schliemann attempted to link descriptions in the *Iliad* to his finds. Pots with faces on them were ingeniously linked with Athena as the patron deity of Troy by interpreting her epithet 'glaukopis' as meaning 'owl-faced' rather than the more usual 'bright-eyed'. Similarly, tall two-handled cups were identified with Homer's 'depas amphikypellon' (Schliemann 1880: 299–302). Although Schliemann's belief in the literal truth in Homer was extreme, and doubted at the time, it does reveal a wider sense that textual evidence should be given priority in interpreting archaeological remains.

One of the reasons that Schliemann returned to Troy in 1878 was to dispel doubts about his claim to have found Priam's Troy. One journalist dismissively referred to 'Priam's Pigsty' and was not the only one to comment on the small size of the settlement (Allen 1999: 185). By then Schliemann had settled his dispute with the Ottoman Empire over Priam's Treasure by paying a large fine. He had negotiated a new permit with the help of the British Ambassador in Constantinople, Sir Austen Henry Layard, who had become famous as the excavator of Nimrud and Nineveh (Traill 1995: 182). The second phase of excavations at Troy was markedly different in character because Schliemann began to collaborate more extensively with the archaeologists and scientists of the day, including German prehistorian and pathologist Rudolf Virchow, Émile Burnouf, director of the French School at Athens and, from 1882, Wilhelm Dörpfeld, from the German Archaeological Institute. Schliemann's 1880 book *Ilios* includes Virchow's measurements of a skull, an early use of craniometry in Aegean archaeology. The book has a more scientific tone in general, describing the different levels of Hissarlik in turn, including the Third City as the city burnt at the end of the Trojan War. It was only in 1890, the year of Schliemann's death, that discoveries of Mycenaean pottery in higher levels showed that these were candidates for the Homeric levels (Schuchhardt 1891: 323–49).

Dörpfeld's experience at Olympia had given him a training in the methods of archaeology and he brought a clearer understanding of stratigraphy to the work at Troy. He continued Schliemann's work after his death, publishing the first accurate section of Troy in his account of his work, establishing the sixth city with its Mycenaean pottery and newly discovered circuit walls as the Homeric city (Figure 7) (Dörpfeld 1902). Schliemann had understood that there were different layers but had relied on recording the depths of objects to assign them to different cities. He assumed, wrongly, that each city occupied a uniform depth in the mound of Hissarlik. Rather than excavating each layer in turn, stratigraphically, he at times had his men quarry through the mound (using iron bars, not dynamite as is often claimed). Nevertheless Schliemann did both keep and record the position of pots and other small finds, which was not always the practice at the time. But claims that Schliemann was 'the true founder of archaeological method' (Casson 1939: 225) are problematic because his methods only improved as he started to collaborate with more experienced excavators. Instead it was the mound of Hissarlik that helped foster better archaeological methods in the Aegean because of its complex stratigraphy. What Schliemann contributed was a huge labour force and a developing model of scientific collaboration, combined with impressively rapid publication.

What remained of Hissarlik was subsequently excavated by a team from the University of Cincinnati led by Carl Blegen in 1932–8. He declared: 'From the start the excavations at Troy were planned as a work of sober, serious research, and there was no compulsion to recover objects of startling or sensational character with high publicity value' (Blegen et al. 1950: 6). He maintained Schliemann and Dörpfeld's levels but refined them, particularly through the development of a clearer pottery typology. The previous typology had been worked out by Hubert Schmidt (1902b) on the basis of the finds which Schliemann had given to Berlin. Although Schliemann was innovative in inviting scientists to examine various finds such as human remains and metals, Blegen's team introduced zooarchaeology to Troy, and the results from various specialists were published in a four-volume site report. The discovery of horse bones in Troy VII was explained in terms of Indo-European invaders, showing the coalescence of new archaeological methods with older styles of interpretation (Blegen et al. 1953: 10). Blegen's aim had been to treat Troy as a prehistoric Anatolian site but he too was drawn into the Homeric Question. A burnt destruction level with a handful of arrows and weapons in it became associated with the Trojan War. This was Troy VIIa, contemporary with Late Helladic IIIB on the Greek mainland.

Apart from the finds at Troy, few Mycenaean objects were excavated on the Anatolian mainland until the 1960s. One exception was the cemetery of Pitane

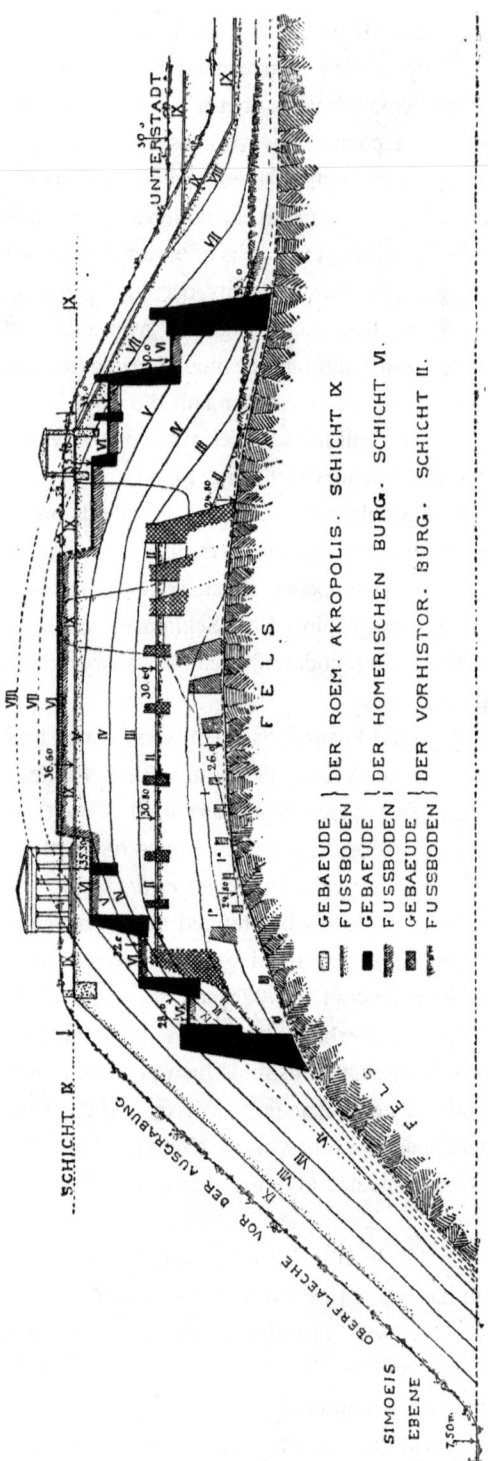

Figure 7 Section drawing of the mound of Hissarlik (Dörpfeld 1902: fig. 6).

(Çandarli), excavated in the nineteenth century by the director of the Imperial Museum, Hamdi Bey. A stirrup jar from this excavation entered the collection (Perrot and Chipiez 1894b: 390; Horejs 2014: 265). There was extensive exploration of Greek and Roman sites along the coast such as Ephesus, explored by British then Austrian archaeologists and Miletus, explored by French and German teams. It was only after the Second World War that significant Bronze Age remains were excavated at these sites. Since they appear to relate to cities mentioned in the Boğazköy archive, Apasa and Millawanda, they have become important parts of the Ahhiyawa Question.

5.2 Dodecanese

The Dodecanese were part of the Ottoman Empire until 1912, when they were annexed by Italy. Hence the first significant Mycenaean site excavated in the Ottoman Empire was on the island of Rhodes. Vice-consul Alfred Biliotti's excavations at Ialysos were part of a long history of extraction of Greek antiquities from the Ottoman Empire. Biliotti had started excavating with Auguste Salzmann at ancient Kamiros in 1859, where they found mainly first millennium BC Greek material. The British Museum had helped obtain a firman and funded the excavation which largely took place in 1863–4 (Salmon 2019). A handful of Bronze Age antiquities entered the collection at this time but were not recognised as such until later. In 1868 Charles Newton instructed Biliotti to locate the cemetery of Ialysos, which he did, on the hill of Moschou Vounara. Pleased with the contents of the four chamber tombs excavated by Biliotti there, Newton secured funding for further excavations from 1870 to 1872 from the art critic John Ruskin. The British Museum often relied on private donations to fund excavations.

In total Biliotti excavated forty-eight rock-cut chamber tombs on Moschou Vounara and nearby Makra Vounara for the British Museum (Mee 1982). In general the tombs were not drawn but Biliotti did keep a record of tomb groups, most likely at the instigation of Newton. The material was mainly pottery although gold jewellery, glass beads, bronze weapons, sealstones and, importantly, three Egyptian scarabs were also found. The material was rapidly put on display at the British Museum, and Schliemann was shown the Ialysos material when he visited London to put his Trojan finds on display in 1877. It was at this time that Newton pointed out the similarities of the pottery with Mycenae, which he declared 'almost identical' (Newton 1880: 284, 294). The Ialysos material was widely discussed in nineteenth-century publications on Mycenaean art. The octopus designs on several pots invited speculation about the evolution of art since they were more stylised than the naturalistic gold octopus plaques from Mycenae. The British Museum also acquired Mycenaean pottery from the islands of Kalymnos and Karpathos in the nineteenth century. They were obtained from local excavators by William Paton, who had travelled around the Aegean and married the daughter of the mayor of Kalymnos (Paton 1887; Gill 2011b: 211).

Following the Italian invasion of the Dodecanese in 1912 a permanent archaeological mission was established under the leadership of Amedeo Maiuri in order to undertake research on all periods. On Rhodes further Mycenaean tombs were excavated at Ialysos by Maiuri (1926) and Giulio Jacopi (1931). Other Mycenaean chamber tomb cemeteries on the island were mapped by Inglieri (1936). The Italian archaeological mission was closely linked to the Fascist regime and archaeologists were encouraged to publish their finds rapidly to demonstrate Italian control over the island (Salmon 2018: 158). Some of their finds are now in Florence, although the majority remained in Rhodes (Benzi 2009). A new archaeological museum was founded in the hospital of the Knights of Saint John, a medieval building which was restored as part of an effort to rediscover the island's supposed Italian heritage (Orlandi 2022). The islands remained under Italian administration until 1947, when they were relinquished as part of the peace treaty signed at the end of the Second World War.

5.3 Peloponnese and Central Greece

Antiquarian interest in the Peloponnese (also known as the Morea in the early modern period) and central Greece predates Greek Independence. Before and after this time, travellers frequently used Pausanias' *Description of Greece* as a guidebook. The second-century geographer visited places including Mycenae, Tiryns and Orchomenos. His descriptions acted as a framework for interpreting these sites, such as use of the term 'Treasury' to describe tholos tombs. The first known traveller from western Europe to visit Mycenae was Cyriacus of Ancona in 1448 (Driessen and Kalantzopoulou 2024: 3). Cyriacus travelled across the Eastern Mediterranean in search of ancient remains and so can be regarded as one of the first antiquarians. The French scholar André de Monceaux visited Tiryns, and perhaps Mycenae, in 1669, while on a mission to collect coins and manuscripts for the Académie des Inscriptions et Belles Lettres (Moore *et al.* 2014: 3). From 1700 onwards there are more frequent records of visits by travellers, starting with Francesco Vandeyk, an engineer taking part in a cadastral survey of the Morea during a brief period when it was held by the Venetians (Lavery and French 2003: 1–2).

Mycenae became a focus of activity at the start of the nineteenth century. A number of artists drew the Lion Gate and Treasury of Atreus. Gell (1810) published a detailed and scholarly account of his visits with plans and drawings of both Tiryns and Mycenae. Colonel Leake also visited both sites in 1804 and noted the 'extreme antiquity' of the remains at Mycenae (Leake 1830: 385; Moore *et al.* 2014: 74–6). At around the same time Lord Elgin was able to obtain permission to take sculpture from the Treasury of Atreus. Its columns were then removed in 1810 by the governor of the Morea, Veli Pasha, who presented them to the visiting Marquis of Sligo. These adorned the side of Sligo's country house in Ireland until they were presented to the British Museum in 1905, reuniting them with the sculptures acquired from Elgin a century earlier (Pryce 1928: 18–24).[6] Veli Pasha also uncovered the Tomb of Clytemnestra and so could be regarded as the first excavator at Mycenae (Neumeier 2017). Mycenaean pottery, as well as sculpture, started to be collected at this time too. Thomas Burgon, who visited Mycenae in 1809, collected pottery sherds from the area and acquired a stirrup jar in Athens (Figure 8).[7] He later described the pottery of Mycenae and Cyclopean architecture as belonging to the 'Heroic Age' (Burgon 1847). Edward Clarke was given a stirrup jar by the British vice-consul in Argos, which he illustrated in his account of his travels and described as a 'libatory vessel' (Clarke 1814: 662).

The Morea Expedition, which began in 1828, marked the intervention of French forces in the Greek War of Independence. In a tradition going back to the campaigns of Napoleon Bonaparte, a scientific mission accompanied the army. The associated publications described the ancient remains of the Peloponnese, Attica and the Cyclades, as well as their natural history and geography. Detailed maps were also produced. As part of this effort, the remains of Mycenae and Tiryns were mapped in detail and various features drawn and described, but no excavations are recorded (Blouet 1833: 147–56). In other cases, such as Pylos, the remains associated with Homer were of a later date.

The first recorded excavation at Tiryns occurred in 1831, although it only lasted one day (Schiering 2010). It was undertaken by Friedrich Thiersch and Alexandros Rangavis, a founding member of the Archaeological Society of Athens. The Archaeological Society was also involved in early excavations at Mycenae, when Kyriakos Pittakis cleared the entrance at the Lion Gate in 1841 (Iakovidis and French 2003: 11). The rights to excavate at Mycenae remained with the Archaeological Society, although Schliemann's first excavation there with a few workmen in 1874 was undertaken without permission from them or the government. When he was forced to stop after a week, during which he made soundings across the site, he moved on to the nearby Argive Heraion for

---

[6] British Museum GR 1816,0610.180; 1816,0610.177; 1816,0610.204; 1816,0610.224 (Elgin); GR 1905,1105.1-3 (Sligo).
[7] Later donated to the British Museum: GR 1842,0728.833.

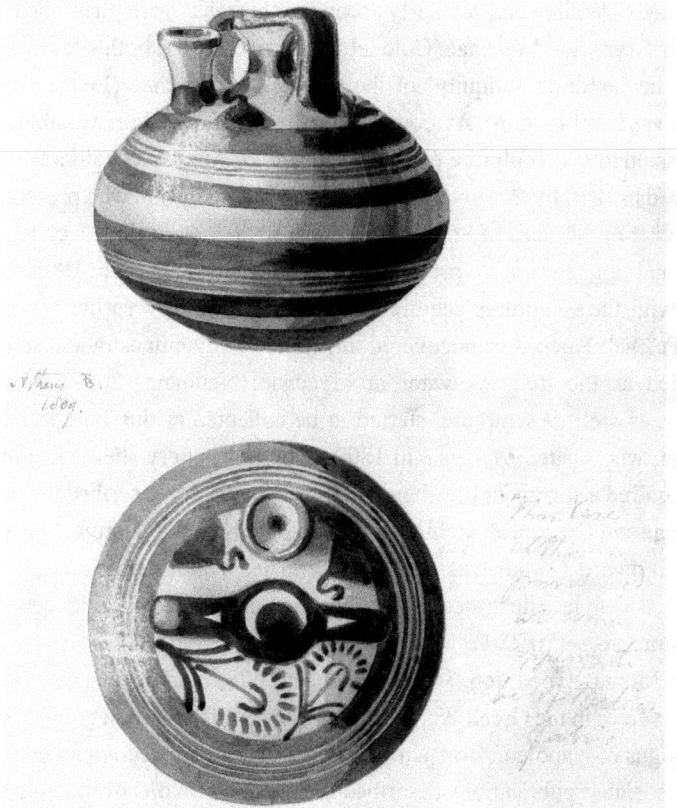

Figure 8 Unpublished drawing by Thomas Burgon of a stirrup jar acquired in Athens, 1809. Burgon Archive drawing no. 241. © Ashmolean Museum, University of Oxford.

a day's excavation (Traill 1995: 128). He subsequently helped to fund the Society's clearance of later buildings from the Athens Acropolis as a way to curry favour.

In 1876 Schliemann was granted permission from the Greek government to excavate at Mycenae, Tiryns and Orchomenos (Traill 1995: 143). These were all places with mythical associations mentioned by Pausanias. After spending a week digging soundings in Tiryns, he moved on to Mycenae. The Archaeological Society had agreed to allow Schliemann to excavate there on its behalf, under the supervision of Panagiotis Stamatakis, who was also a member of the Ephoria and an experienced excavator. Sophia Schliemann also supervised the work and the steadily growing team of workmen, which came to number over 100. Excavations began in August at the Tomb of Clytemnestra and an area inside the citadel walls by the Lion Gate. Schliemann decided to dig here in search of the graves of Agamemnon and his followers since Pausanias said that they were buried within the city walls following their murder on their return from the Trojan War. The soundings in this area had also proved promising (Schliemann 1878: 59–61). It is not clear if Pausanias was referring to this area but Schliemann's literal approach soon paid dividends as he started to find a circular space, which he termed the Agora, and carved stele which looked like gravestones.

The Shaft Graves, which consisted of rock-cut chambers accessed by long vertical shafts, were not uncovered until November 1876. Schliemann was responsible for the excavation of five graves, each richer than the previous one. All contained multiple burials adorned with gold ornaments and accompanied by weapons and other precious grave goods. Shaft Grave IV was the first to contain gold masks covering the faces of the deceased. It was this grave which prompted Schliemann to send a telegram to the King of Greece to declare his success in finding the graves of Agamemnon and his followers (Schliemann 1878: 365). A fifth was excavated in the following days and contained the mask which has become known as the 'Mask of Agamemnon' although was not identified as such by Schliemann (Figure 9).[8] Satisfied that he had found what

Figure 9 Photograph of the Mask of Agamemnon. Sir Arthur Evans Archive AJE/3/1/15/18/1. © Ashmolean Museum, University of Oxford.

---

[8] National Archaeological Museum, Athens 624.

he was looking for, Schliemann left. In just over two weeks he had cleared five graves containing nineteen individuals and thousands of grave goods (Karo 1930). A sixth shaft grave was excavated in the following year by Stamatakis (Papazoglou-Manioudaki *et al.* 2009: 234–42).

The discoveries at Mycenae caused an immediate sensation, both within Greece and internationally. Schliemann had been sending regular updates to *The Times* in London about his work at Mycenae (Meyer 1958: 53–66). In December 1876 a long article appeared in *The Times* headed 'The Tomb of Agamemnon' with a detailed account written by Schliemann of his discoveries of the first four graves. The following year the finds were put on display by the Archaeological Society, as arranged by Stamatakis (Konstantinidi-Syvridi and Paschalidis 2019: 116–8). Schliemann's own account of his discoveries appeared in 1878, with a foreword by the prime minister of the United Kingdom, William Gladstone. They had met when Schliemann presented his discoveries at Mycenae to the Society of Antiquaries in London. Although a few scholars had doubted the antiquity of the remains, suggesting the masks were Byzantine or later, the discoveries at Mycenae convinced most people that there was some truth in the Homeric myths (Gardner 1880). Homer's epithet for Mycenae, 'rich in gold', seemed to have been dramatically demonstrated, since over 15 kg of gold had been found in the graves. There was more doubt about the identities of those buried. Even Gladstone thought it unlikely that the murderers of Agamemnon would provide him with such a rich burial, and most scholars rejected the link altogether. Instead Schliemann's results demonstrated that that there was a 'heroic' or 'pre-hellenic' stage in Greek history which could yield spectacular finds.

The effect of Schliemann's excavation at Mycenae on prehistoric archaeology in Greece can be gauged by the number of tholos and chamber tombs excavated in the succeeding years. In many cases these would have been known locally but what Schliemann had demonstrated was that it was worth the expense of investigating such remains. Before this, for the Archaeological Society and others, the focus had been on classical Greek sites. In 1878, for instance, Stamatakis excavated a tholos tomb near the Argive Heraion whose entrance had been discovered by a local villager in 1872 (Stamatakis 1878). The previous year Stamatakis had excavated another large tomb at Spata in Attica, and a smaller tomb nearby, which had been revealed by a landslide. Its contents were not intact but some pottery and other finds were still in situ (Koumanoudis and Kastorchis 1877). Efthymios Kastorchis, a prominent member of the Archaeological Society, also explored chamber tombs at Nauplion with Ioannis Kondakis in 1878, noting their resemblance to those at Spata. Some had already been discovered by a local farmer (Kondakis and Kastorchis 1878).

The first intact tholos tomb burial was excavated in 1879 by Habbo Lolling from the German Archaeological Institute at Menidi in Acharnes, Attica. As he noted in his report, the site had been known for some years but the other excavations of Mycenaean tombs had aroused interest in it (Lolling 1880: 1). Finds included glass jewellery, sealstones and a carved ivory box. Six skeletons were also found which proved that such tholoi were indeed tombs rather than treasuries (Tsountas and Manatt 1897: 6).

In 1880 Schliemann turned to the third site on his permit, the tholos tomb at Orchomenos. This had been described by Pausanias as the Treasury of Minyas and had long attracted attention. Colonel Leake visited and tried to resolve Pausanias' description of a domed roof with a keystone with the remaining architecture, noting that 'An excavation will some day determine this question' (Leake 1830: 379). Schliemann did not uncover burials but found an impressive carved slab and grey pottery which he named 'Minyan Ware' as well as Mycenaean sherds (Schliemann 1881a, 1881b). In the following decade several more Mycenaean tombs were excavated. Valerios Stais excavated the tholos at Thorikos and chamber tombs at Epidauros (Petrochilos 1992: 19–21). In 1889 Christos Tsountas excavated the tholos at Vapheio in Laconia and found an intact burial beneath the floor (Tsountas 1889). With the skeleton were found around thirty sealstones, some from Crete, and two gold cups with repousse scenes of bull-catching which became known as the 'Vapheio Cups'. They rapidly went on display in the newly opened National Archaeological Museum.[9]

Tiryns and Mycenae continued to receive attention in the wake of these spectacular mortuary finds. Schliemann excavated at Tiryns for two seasons in 1884 and 1885, with Wilhelm Dörpfeld. They uncovered the plan of a building which they regarded as the palace on the citadel, using the Homeric term 'megaron' to describe the central rooms. This area, they decided, also following Homer, was the men's quarters with the smaller women's quarters nearby (Schliemann 1885). In 1886 Christos Tsountas excavated the remains of the palace at Mycenae, which was less well preserved because part of the acropolis had eroded away (Tsountas 1888). He continued to excavate in the surrounding area, revealing a large chamber tomb cemetery. Meanwhile in Athens, the excavations by Panagiotis Kavvadias on the Acropolis started to reveal Mycenaean remains (Tsountas and Manatt 1897: 8). This meant that the settlements of the Mycenaean period began to be better known too. Further Mycenaean settlement remains were discovered by an American team at the Argive Heraion in 1893 although the main focus was the later temple (Waldstein

---

[9] National Archaeological Museum, Athens 1758 and 1759.

1902–5). In the same year André de Ridder (1894) excavated the palace at Gla in the middle of the recently drained Copais basin. Although remains had been noted here as early as 1805, the excavation of other Mycenaean settlements allowed it to be identified as such (Lane 2021).

By 1893, Christos Tsountas had enough evidence to paint a picture of the Mycenaean civilisation, with both mortuary and settlement sites, and a range of art objects. For the earlier stages of the civilisation, he looked across the Aegean to Troy and the Cyclades (Tsountas and Manatt 1897: 256–7). In the twentieth century, attention shifted to the origins of the Mycenaean civilisation on the mainland itself. Wilhelm Dörpfeld had returned to Tiryns in 1905, with Georg Karo and Kurt Müller, and the German Archaeological Institute excavations continued there until the outbreak of the First World War, resuming again in the 1920s (Schiering 2010). An important discovery was the Early Bronze Age *Rundbau*, a monumental circular building, in 1912 (Maran 2016). Orchomenos was excavated in 1903 and 1905 by Adolf Furtwängler and Heinrich Bulle for the Bavarian Academy of Sciences, where early round buildings were also discovered (Bulle 1907). Furtwängler identified a type of lustrous pottery which he termed 'Urfirnis' in the early levels and Minyan Ware was recognised in the pre-Mycenaean levels. Rather than focussing on palaces and tombs, these excavations started to reveal the layers of occupation beneath Mycenaean sites.

Tumulus sites were to become increasingly important for the question of origins since they contained multiple phases of occupation going back to the Middle and Early Bronze Age, but without the disturbance by later architecture seen at palatial sites. One of the first tumuli to be excavated was Aphidna in Attica (Wide 1896; Hielte 2023). This was also the first prehistoric Aegean site to be excavated by a Swedish archaeologist, Sam Wide. Within the tumulus, which Wide correctly identified as belonging to the start of the Middle Bronze Age, were thirteen later graves, including a number of shaft graves, although without the splendid finds of Mycenae. In the absence of a Swedish School of Archaeology, Wide worked closely with the German Archaeological Institute, receiving training from Wilhelm Dörpfeld. Another prehistoric tumulus, Magoula Balomenou at Chaeronea was excavated at the turn of the century by Georgios Sotiriadis (1908).

These sites provided important comparative material for the tumulus at Korakou, excavated from 1915 by Carl Blegen, who was participating in the American School excavations at Corinth nearby. At Korakou, Blegen discovered a complete sequence of Bronze Age pottery, having excavated the mound stratigraphically under the guidance of Alan Wace (Blegen 1921; Tzonou-Herbst 2015). It was this which enabled him, with Alan Wace, to propose a classification of Helladic pottery from mainland sites (Wace and

Blegen 1918). Lustrous Urfirnis pottery was grouped with other wares as Early Helladic, while Minyan Ware was included with Matt-Painted pottery as Middle Helladic. These provided the precursors to Late Helladic Mycenaean pottery. Blegen went on to excavate another multi-period site, Zygouries in the Argolid, where an extensive Early Helladic settlement was found (Blegen 1928). Eutresis, near Thebes, was another tumulus site with a long history of occupation. This was excavated in the 1920s by the American Hetty Goldman, one of the few women to lead an excavation in this period (Goldman 1931). The importance of these pre-Mycenaean sites for their excavators was that they helped to confirm the Bronze Age sequence and shed light on the inhabitants of Greece before the Mycenaean civilisation. The change in pottery types seen between Early and Middle Helladic led to suggestions of some kind of invasion (Blegen 1928: 186; Goldman 1931: 233). As Wace and Blegen (1918: 189) argued, 'the period of Minyan Ware indicates the introduction of a new cultural strain, the origin of which is not yet clear'. This fitted into the culture-historical thinking which characterised European prehistory at this time. This was epitomised by Gordon Childe, who had worked with Wace and Blegen during the First World War and later wrote about these sites in *The Dawn of European Civilisation* (Childe 1957: 66–83).

Mycenae too was subject to continuing debate about the origins of its inhabitants. Alan Wace, director of the British School at Athens, resumed excavations there in 1919, which continued until 1923 (Lamb and Wace 1921; Wace *et al.* 1923). One of his contributions was to use the refined pottery chronology to establish a sequence of construction for citadel and surrounding tombs. He demonstrated that Grave Circle A predated the building of the citadel wall and was part of a larger cemetery. His dating of the tholoi resulted in a serious disagreement with Sir Arthur Evans about the relative chronology of the mainland and Crete. Wace argued that the Treasury of Atreus post-dated the destruction at Knossos, showing that the archaeology of mainland Greece was partly independent of Crete (Figure 10). As a result Evans' 'pan-Minoan' theory of mainland conquest by Crete in the Shaft Grave period became less tenable. This disagreement continued for the next two decades and was only really settled in Wace's favour with the decipherment of Linear B. Wace resumed excavations at Mycenae in 1939 and continued after the Second World War.

The Argolid continued to be a focus of Mycenaean archaeology in this period. Wilhelm Vollgraf, a Dutch archaeologist, excavated the prehistoric site of Aspis near Argos and the associated Deiras cemetery in 1902–4 (Vollgraf 1904; Papadimitriou *et al.* 2020). Carl Blegen resumed excavations at the Argive Heraion in the 1920s, finding the Bronze Age settlement Prosymna (Blegen 1937). He also continued excavations in the chamber tomb

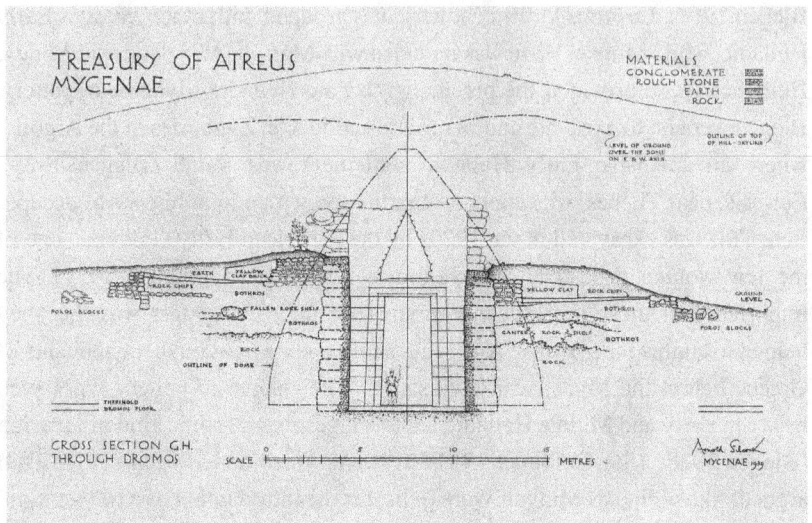

Figure 10 Section drawing of the Treasury of Atreus at Mycenae. Drawn by A. Silcock. Mycenae Archive MCNE-2-2-03-03. © Faculty of Classics, University of Cambridge.

cemetery started by Stamatakis. A number of sites were excavated in the 1920s by Swedish archaeologists led by Otto Frödin and Axel Persson. They began excavations in 1922 at Asine, a Mycenaean citadel which was mentioned in the *Iliad* (Frödin and Persson 1938: 15). The main backer of the dig was the Crown Prince of Sweden, who also took part. In 1926 Persson was invited by the Ephor Nikolaos Bertos to dig a tholos tomb at Dendra whose entrance had been uncovered by local villagers. Intact burials of three individuals accompanied by jewellery, sealstones, bronze weapons and two gold cups, one with an octopus design, were found in graves below the floor.[10] Persson regarded these as a king, queen and princess (Persson 1931: 8–18). Further tombs were excavated by the Ephor and Swedish team in subsequent years. The 1939 season saw work in the nearby citadel of Midea where a Mycenaean palace was identified before the Second World War intervened (Persson 1942).

Alongside the improvements in pottery typologies and excavation methods, the twentieth century saw a continuation of interest in Homeric sites. As well as the ongoing excavations at Tiryns, Mycenae and Orchomenos, new sites were discovered. In 1906 a Mycenaean palace, identified as the House of Kadmos or Kadmeia, was discovered under modern Thebes by Antonios Keramopoullos (1909; Aravantinos 2006). Among the important finds were fragments of wall

---

[10] Octopus cup: National Archaeological Museum, Athens 7341.

painting showing a procession of elaborately dressed female figures. The palace's excavation had to take place piecemeal until 1929 because of the modern buildings above. In 1910 a Mycenaean building was uncovered near Sparta, beneath the later shrine to Menelaus and Helen, although it was not identified as a palace by the excavators (Dawkins and Woodward 1910). This was part of a broader project on this area started by the British School at Athens which focussed mainly on the later sanctuaries. The Mycenaean palace at nearby Ayios Vasileos was only discovered in 2009.

One Homeric site which had not been located despite various attempts to identify it was Pylos. The toponym was still associated with the Bay of Navarino in the southwest Peloponnese and various sites in the area had been identified with Nestor's Palace. Schliemann made a number of trial excavations at one candidate in 1888 (Blegen 1966: 3). In 1907–8 Wilhelm Dörpfeld excavated three tholos tombs further up the coast at Kakovatos which still contained rich grave goods. He identified an associated building as Nestor's Palace. Attention began to shift back to Pylos with the excavation of two tholos tombs in the vicinity by Ephor Konstantinos Kourouniotis following reports of looting. This suggested that a Mycenaean settlement was yet to be found in this area. Kourouniotis initiated a survey in 1927–8 in collaboration with Carl Blegen in order to locate further sites. The prime candidate became the ridge of Ano Englianos where the local landowner had already informed the Ephorate about archaeological remains (Davis 2015: 209). After disagreements with the American School, Carl Blegen had turned to Troy, and only started excavations at Pylos in 1939. He immediately discovered substantial walls, painted plaster and a cache of Linear B tablets (Blegen and Rawson 1966: 1–7). By the time the first season finished, over 600 Linear B tablets had been found in what was identified as the Archive Room. When the excavation resumed in 1952, the Linear B tablets had been published in preliminary form, which aided their decipherment. Excavations continued until 1964. Although methods of excavation and standards of publication had improved dramatically since 1876, the long tradition of excavating at sites associated with Greek mythology continued.

5.4 Cycladic Islands

The trajectory of prehistoric Aegean archaeology in the Cyclades was different from the mainland because of the character of the archaeological remains and associated objects. Even before the Kingdom of Greece was established, of which the Cyclades were a constituent part, Cycladic figurines and other objects were being dug up from graves and exported. The British Museum collection includes both Cycladic and Mycenaean figurines from the collection of Percy Smythe, Sixth Viscount Strangford, who was ambassador to the Sublime Porte in 1820–4. One of the Mycenaean figurines was acquired on Melos in 1821, and three Cycladic figurines were almost certainly acquired at the same time, probably from a dealer on Mykonos (Pryce 1928: 8–12; Galanakis 2013: 199).[11] Thomas Burgon, who operated as a merchant in the Aegean, excavated Cycladic pottery from Melos and a marble figurine from Syros, acquired 1809, which also entered the British Museum collection (Pryce 1928: 10).[12] A contemporary drawing also survives but this was not published at the time (Figure 11). A French naval officer, Jules de Blosseville, acquired Cycladic vases on Melos around 1831, which he donated to the National Ceramics Museum at Sèvres (Brongniart and Riocreux 1845: 52–3). These probably came from graves in the area of Phylakopi, discovered in 1830 (Atkinson et al. 1904: 24). Around the same time Friedrich Thiersch acquired two marble figurines on Paros while part of an official Bavarian delegation to Greece. In his publication of them Thiersch (1835) followed classical tradition in identifying the figures as Carian, and later donated them to the Badisches Landesmuseum in Karlsruhe.[13] Although these are early examples, the flow of Cycladic objects out of Greece into western European collections continued despite the 1834 antiquities law, with most lacking a provenance beyond an island of origin.

When the first General Ephor of Greece, Ludwig Ross, toured the islands in the 1830s, he witnessed islanders digging Early Bronze Age tombs and in some cases acquired their contents. On Ios in 1837 he and his travelling companions were shown the location where a hellenistic sarcophagus known as the 'Tomb of Homer' had been found in the eighteenth century. The Russian naval officer who removed the sarcophagus, Graf Pasch van Krienen, had noted marble bowls and obsidian blades in the same location (Ross 1840: 161; Fotiadis 2016: 97). The landowner showed the contents of other graves, including obsidian blades and marble figurines, which had been opened more recently in the same location. George Finlay, who was accompanying Ross, purchased figurines from Ios, which he described as 'rude', and other objects. Ross too bought a figurine, which is now in Copenhagen (Arnott 1990).[14] Ross (1837: 408–9) compared the figurines he had seen on Ios and Thera with those published by Thiersch, describing them as 'vorhellenisch' (pre-Hellenic). He suggested that Thera in particular, where he had excavated later graves, clearly concealed many ancient remains under its layer of pumice.

---

[11] British Museum GR 1864,0220.32 (Mycenaean figurine) and GR 1863,0213.1; GR 1863,0213.2; GR 1863,0213.3 (Cycladic figurines).
[12] British Museum GR 1842,0728.616.   [13] Karlsruhe B 839 and B 840.
[14] Nationalmuseet Abb 139.

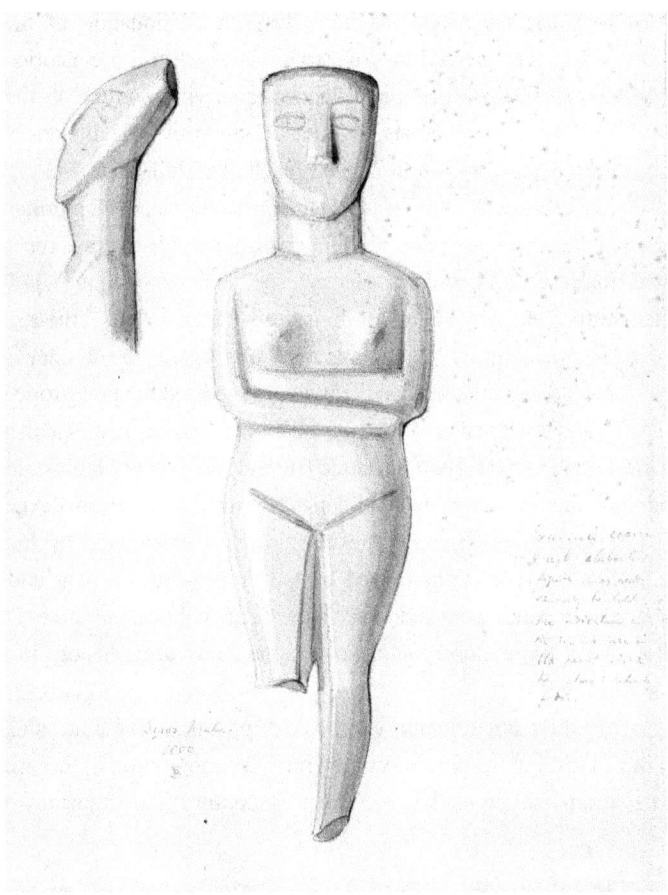

Figure 11 Unpublished drawing by Thomas Burgon of a Cycladic figurine acquired on Syros, 1809. Burgon Archive drawing no. 298. © Ashmolean Museum, University of Oxford.

There is circumstantial evidence that members of the Morea Expedition excavated Bronze Age levels on Thera in 1829 and found prehistoric pottery (Tzachili 2005: 234). One of their number also donated a kernos from Melos to the Sèvres Museum (Bosanquet 1897: 60). Thera was of particular interest to scientists because of the volcanic activity there. It was also already being extensively excavated for its pumice, which was used to make concrete, most notably in the construction of the Suez Canal. These excavations had uncovered antiquities, and there were already collections of antiquities in private hands when Ross visited in the 1830s and 1840s (Tzachili 2005: 242). The collectors were members of the island's ruling classes who had developed an interest in its antiquities and history. When the Thera volcano erupted in 1866, a French scientific mission was despatched to study the island, in some ways a continuation of the Morea Expedition. When they arrived they became interested in a prehistoric building which had already been revealed by islanders quarrying pumice on the islet of Therasia. Two of the local collectors, Sigouras Alaphouzos and Nikolaos Nomikos, conducted an excavation on behalf of the French (Tzachili 2005: 243–5; Fotiadis 2016: 101). The classical archaeologist on the mission François Lenormant (1866: 432) regarded the associated pottery as Phoenician, since Herodotus recorded that Thera was formerly a Phoenician colony. The geologist Fouqué (1879), who supervised further excavations in 1867, instead turned to the three-age system and classified the remains as belonging to the Stone Age, in the absence of bronze (Figure 12). He also established that the building predated the prehistoric eruption of the island and assigned it a date of 2000 BCE using geological methods. Subsequent excavations in 1870 by Emile Burnouf did recover bronze, leading to his recognition that the associated antiquities belonged to the Bronze Age. As Iris Tzachili (2005: 233) observes, this excavation was abandoned by the French because of funding restrictions caused by the Franco-Prussian war and did not resume because the finds were incidental to the Greek political narrative. The Thera excavations were more closely aligned with the study of prehistory in northern Europe at this time.

Some of the first documented excavations on other Cycladic islands took place in the 1880s, but in some ways they mark a continuation of the small-scale local excavations that go back to earlier in the century. Two figurines, a harpist

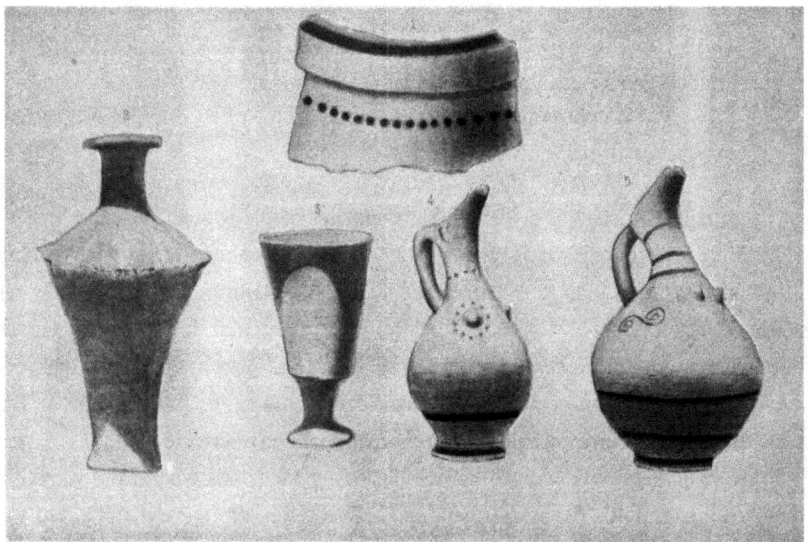

Figure 12 Vases from Thera (Fouqué 1879: pl. XLI).

and an aulete, were found in a grave in Keros in 1883 and acquired by the Archaeological Society before being transferred to the National Archaeological Museum (Köhler 1884).[15] James Theodore Bent travelled around the Cyclades with his wife Mabel in 1883–4 and decided to excavate at Antiparos, opening forty cist graves (Bent 1885: 403–10). The cemeteries were pointed out to him by islanders, who also took part in the excavations. Finds were donated to the British Museum, including ceramics, obsidian tools and figurines. Bent suggested that they must predate the finds at Thera, and so belong to the 'remotest antiquity'. In 1885 Georg Ferdinand Dümmler visited Amorgos and commissioned excavations, although his ostensible aim was to view collections (Dümmler 1886; Galanakis 2013). A prominent local collector and antiquarian was a priest, Dimitrios Prasinos, who showed the Bents round the island. Prasinos was also a landowner and excavator, who later worked with Christos Tsountas. Before the passing of the 1899 law, landowners such as Prasinos were entitled to dig for antiquities but the state should have issued a permit and had first refusal on their sale. Instead it was travellers and Athens-based antiquities dealers who tended to buy these objects.

By the time Tsountas conducted his own excavations in the Cyclades on behalf of the Greek state in the 1890s, the major cemeteries had all been extensively disturbed. Tsountas' work at Amorgos, Syros, Paros and Sifnos differed from previous excavators in that he documented his discoveries extensively and his finds went to the National Archaeological Museum (Tsountas 1898, 1899). As a result he is credited with identifying the Cycladic civilisation. On Syros he also undertook the first documented excavation at the settlement site of Kastri in 1898. Digging had started at the nearby cemetery of Chalandriani by 1861, but Tsountas uncovered 540 graves here in 1898 (Marthari 1998: 17–18). The first settlement site to be excavated, from 1896 to 1899, was Phylakopi on Melos, by members of the British School at Athens. They had initially come to Melos in search of classical remains but turned their attention to Phylakopi because it was described by Dümmler and objects from the cemetery there were known from the Athens antiquities market (Atkinson *et al.* 1904: 1–2). From the start it was of interest because it had both Cycladic and Mycenaean remains, so offered a stratified Bronze Age sequence. Duncan Mackenzie was placed in charge of the excavations. He had studied in Munich, Berlin and Vienna, so had a thorough grounding in *Altertumwissenschaft*, but no archaeological experience. Nevertheless he soon gained a reputation as a scientific excavator and kept detailed records of the work there. He also

---

[15] National Archaeological Museum, Athens, 3908 and 3910.

travelled round the Cyclades acquiring antiquities for Arthur Evans at the Ashmolean Museum in Oxford (Momigliano 1999: 16–35).

Cycladic sculpture enjoyed a surge of interest in the first half of the twentieth century in the art world but this was not matched by the pace of research in the islands themselves. The British returned for a further season at Phylakopi in 1909 to make further tests of the stratigraphy. French excavations on Delos, which had always focussed on the classical remains, revealed prehistoric levels on Mount Kynthos underneath the later sanctuaries. Another prolific excavator of Early Cycladic tombs was the Greek anthropologist Klon Stephanos, who worked on Syros and Naxos (Zervos 1957: 2–4; Papazoglou-Manioudaki 2017). The primitivism movement resulted in a re-evaluation of Cycladic sculpture, which was increasingly praised for its simplicity rather than being regarded as ugly. Museums outside Greece continued to collect Cycladic sculpture in the interwar period although the scale of acquisition, and looting, increased in the 1950s and 1960s (Gill and Chippindale 1993: 616). Typological studies lagged behind, with Colin Renfrew's (1969) classification the first serious attempt to establish a systematic framework for the study of figurines.

5.5 Ionian Islands

The Ionian Islands have an entirely different political history from other Greek islands since they were never part of the Ottoman Empire. The conquest of Venice by Napoleon in 1797 saw them become French possessions but they were rapidly taken by the British during the Napoleonic Wars. From 1815 they were formally a British protectorate with their own government and legal system. As in the Aegean, however, the Homeric Question dominated research since Odysseus was king of Ithaca. In 1806 Leake had visited Alalkomenes, the fortified hellenistic site on Mount Aetos which was traditionally associated with Odysseus' Palace: 'I pitched my tent, and remained the whole day examining the ruins, or looking over the topographical passages of the Odyssey, while a party of labourers excavated some ancient sepulchres in the valley' (Leake 1835: 34). His labourers, he noted, did not find anything earlier than Roman coins. Another traveller, John Lee, had more success in 1812, when his hired labourers hit a hellenistic tomb elsewhere on the island. Lee (1849) was also interested in Homeric remains and had sought permission from the commandant of Ithaca to dig. Both recorded that the local inhabitants frequently found antiquities on their land, and so hiring them to look for ancient remains was not a leap of the imagination. The main difference was that the travellers recorded, albeit vaguely, where excavations took place.

On the neighbouring island of Cephallonia the Swiss engineer Philippe de Bosset initiated various road-building projects while acting as governor on behalf of the British. As a result Mycenaean tombs were discovered at Mazarakata in 1813, whose contents he donated to Neuchâtel Museum and probably the local library in Argostoli (Souyoudzoglou-Haywood 1999: 9, 149–50). De Bosset did not publish his finds, although he did describe them in his correspondence, allowing the Neuchâtel finds to be published retrospectively when their significance was finally realised (Brodbeck-Jucker 1986). When the Ephor General Panagiotis Kavvadias excavated further chamber tombs in this location in 1899, he was unaware of the earlier finds. He later excavated two robbed tholoi in the same area (Kavvadias 1912) (Figure 13). A British army officer based on Corfu, James Woodhouse, amassed a large collection of objects, many of which were donated to the British Museum on his death in 1866. They include a Mycenaean dagger said to come from Ithaca (Sandars 1963: 152).[16]

Homeric archaeology continued on the Ionian islands after they were ceded to Greece in 1864. The main difference between archaeology here and elsewhere in the Aegean is that a Mycenaean palace has not to date been found in this area. In 1868, on his first visit to Ithaca, Schliemann too visited Mount Aetos and hired workmen to dig where he thought the palace should be. He identified cremation burials found there with Odysseus and Penelope although these are now known to postdate the Bronze Age (Schliemann 1869: 27–38). Without clear evidence on Ithaca, the search widened to include other islands. From 1900 a wealthy Dutch architect, Adriaan Goekoop, funded a number of excavation projects to answer this question: Panagiotis Kavvadias favoured Cephallonia, his native island; Wilhelm Vollgraf excavated at Polis on Ithaca, where he found Mycenaean sherds; Wilhelm Dörpfeld turned to the island of Leukada as the most likely candidate. There he excavated for a number of years from 1901, finding Early Helladic tumuli but almost no trace of Mycenaean occupation, which did not shake his belief that this was Odysseus' island (Dörpfeld and Goessler 1927). In the 1930s, the British School at Athens, funded by Lord Rennell, continued to explore Ithaca (Rennell Rodd 1933). Sylvia Benton found a number of bronze tripods at the Cave of the Nymphs at Polis, which almost certainly indicated a later hero cult to Odysseus, but little evidence for Mycenaean remains (Benton 1935). Mycenaean sherds also were discovered at Aetos for the first time (Heurtley and Lorimer 1933). Benton and Hilda Lorimer went on to excavate at Zakynthos, where they did find Late Bronze Age remains (Souyoudzoglou-Haywood 1999: 126). The search for Odysseus' Palace continues to the present day (Souyoudzoglou-Haywood 2018).

---

[16] British Museum GR 1868,0110.342.

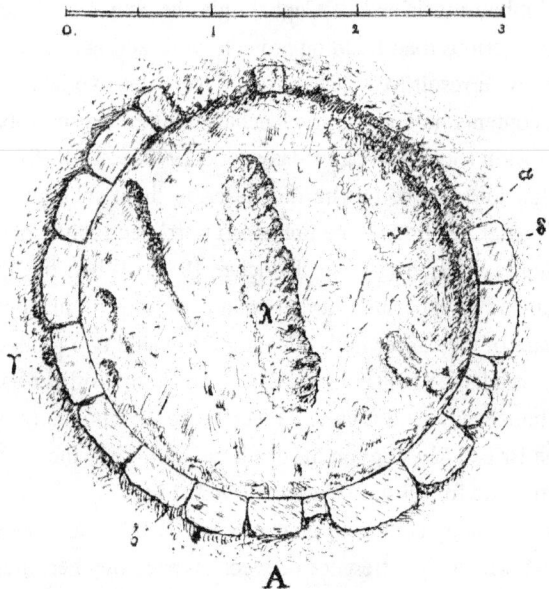

Εἰκ. 1. Θολωτὸς τάφος A. Κάτοψις.

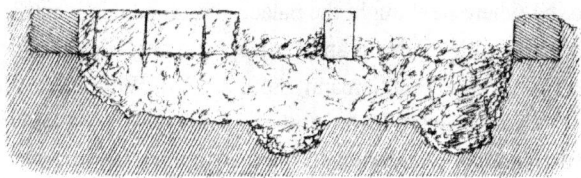

Εἰκ. 2. Θολωτὸς τάφος A. Τομὴ α - β

Εἰκ. 3 Θολωτὸς τάφος A. Τομὴ γ - δ.

Figure 13 Plan and section drawing of tholos tomb at Mazarakata (Kavvadias 1912: figs. 1–3).

5.6 Thessaly

The focus of activity for prehistoric archaeology in Thessaly was initially the area around Volos, where the ancient city of Iolkos was located. Early in the nineteenth century Dodwell identified Homeric Iolkos at Ano Volos, where there are visible

Byzantine remains (Dodwell 1819: 30–31; 1834: 30). In the decades after 1881, when Thessaly became part of Greece, Mycenaean remains were excavated at Dimini, to the west of Volos and Kastro Palaia, now an eastern suburb. Three tholos tombs were excavated in the vicinity of Dimini. First was Lamiospito in 1886, excavated by Habbo Lolling with a local schoolteacher, Eleutherios Kousis (Lolling and Wolters 1886). Schoolteachers and other officials were co-opted by the Ephorate to work on its behalf as Thessaly was absorbed into Greece (Gallis 1979: 2). Valerios Stais excavated a further two tholoi in Dimini, in 1892 and 1901. Christos Tsountas excavated Mycenaean tombs at Kastro between 1900 and 1902. Mycenaean vessels from Pefkakia, on the harbour of Volos, were published by Wolters (1889), who had been able to identify the site after seeing them in a local collection. The site was not excavated until the 1950s. An unlooted tholos containing gold ornaments was excavated at Kapakli in Volos in 1905 by the Ephor Konstantinos Kourouniotis (1906). These finds helped to show the importance of Mycenaean Iolkos, traditionally associated with the hero Jason, although its exact location, whether Volos or Dimini, remained unclear.

The work on Mycenaean tombs resulted in the identification of some of the mounds of Thessaly as Neolithic tell sites (other local terms include *magoula* and *toumba*). Christos Tsountas first excavated in Thessaly in 1899 to investigate the Mycenaean tombs at Marmariani near Larissa (Gallis 1979: 3). On the mound there he saw bone and stone tools as well as what looked like pre-Mycenaean pottery. In 1901 Stais had started to investigate the mound at Dimini which the tholos tomb had been dug into. This turned out to be a large Late Neolithic settlement consisting of several enclosures containing dwellings with distinctive burnished dark-on-white painted vessels (Tsountas 1908: 27–68) (Figure 14). In the same year Tsountas started excavations at nearby Sesklo, where Leake had noted an ancient site when he passed through in 1809 (Leake 1835: 399). Tsountas excavated on the Kastraki hill, finding a settlement with deep stratification which he divided into Earlier and Later Neolithic, with Bronze Age above. Here there were mudbrick buildings with stone footings, monochrome and painted pottery and a large number of figurines. He subsequently finished the excavations of Stais at Dimini in 1903 (Tsountas 1908: 69–104). By the time he wrote up his findings in *The Prehistoric Citadels of Dimini and Sesklo* he had identified sixty-three Neolithic sites, laying the foundations for the study of the Neolithic in Greece (Tsountas 1908: 1–14).

Alan Wace, John Droop and Maurice Thompson from the British School at Athens continued the exploration of Thessaly by digging at a number of Neolithic and Bronze Age mounds: Theotokou in 1907, Zerelia in 1908, Lianokladi and Tsani in 1909, and Tsangli and Rakhmani in 1910 (Wace and

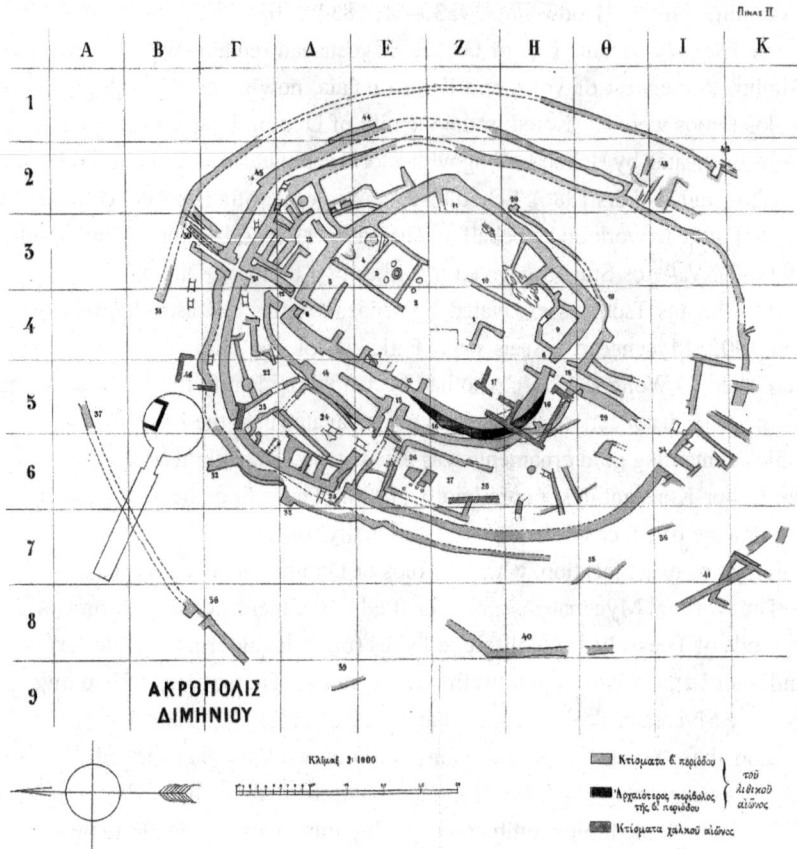

Figure 14 Phased plan of the settlement of Dimini (Tsountas 1908: pl. 2).

Thompson 1912). Their principal aim was to isolate pottery sequences by digging them stratigraphically. They accepted Tsountas' division of the Neolithic into two but defined a number of different types of pottery within each period. Dark-on-light 'Dimini Ware' became one of the characteristic wares of the later Neolithic. They identified a Chalcolithic phase before the Bronze Age which signalled that they regarded Thessaly as more similar to Central Europe than southern Greece. As they concluded: 'Starting with the earliest remains and proceeding in chronological order up to the end of the prehistoric age we saw that North Greece throughout possessed a different culture from the south, and that Mycenaean influence never succeeded in permeating Thessaly, which always continued in a backward and barbarous state of civilisation' (Wace and Thompson 1912: 255). In this way Thessaly came to occupy a role as a precursor of Mycenaean Greece but also a peripheral part of it. From the 1950s a new wave of archaeological research revisited many of these sites and put Thessaly back at the forefront of research on Neolithic Greece (Andreou *et al.* 2001: 261–82).

5.7 Northern Greece and the Islands of the Northern Aegean

Mounds became emblematic of the prehistory of Macedonia. Although they had been observed by earlier travellers, their significance as prehistoric sites was not realised until they started to be excavated in the late nineteenth century. Even then, the existence of hellenistic burial mounds in the landscape alongside prehistoric tell sites meant that it took time to distinguish between them. Léon Heuzey, the French archaeologist, became the first to excavate one of these mounds, finding a built tomb (Heuzey 1860: 171–7). One of the first to excavate a prehistoric mound was the Ottoman archaeologist Theodore Makridis, Makridi Bey, who went on to succeed Hamdi Bey as director of the Imperial Museum at Constantinople. In the late nineteenth century he dug at the mound at Kalamaria (Toumba Thessaloniki) in search of a tomb but rapidly realised its prehistoric character (Palli 2012). He went on to excavate the prehistoric mound of Platanaki but did not publish his results (Wace 1914: 128; Heurtley 1939: 25).

The first publications about the prehistoric mounds of Macedonia relied on surface collections. In 1900 Paul Traeger collected sherds from various mounds and brought them back to Berlin to show Hubert Schmidt, who was also working on the pottery from Troy (Schmidt 1902a; Traeger 1902). This helped to date them to the Bronze Age. Traeger made a distinction between the later Greek conical burial mounds and the flatter settlement sites which he regarded as prehistoric. Alan Wace and Maurice Thompson moved north from Thessaly from 1909 to survey the mounds of Macedonia, proposing a threefold classification which split the settlement *toumbes* into prehistoric and later Greek in date, and created a list of seventy mounds (Wace and Thompson 1909; Wace 1914). The British had established a 'Macedonian Exploration Fund' in 1911 to support further research but war intervened (Gill 2011b: 181–3).

Soon after Greece's territorial gains in the Balkan Wars were ratified in the 1913 Treaty of Constantinople, an Ephor, Georgios Oikonomos, was despatched to take over the archaeological affairs of the area around Thessaloniki. Apostolos Arvanitopoulos, previously Ephor of Thessaly, became the Ephor of the newly conquered region of Central and Western Macedonia, having himself fought in an artillery regiment during the area's capture (Gallis 1979: 8–9). It was the First World War, however, which resulted in the first large-scale excavation of the prehistoric mounds, and many other sites in Macedonia (Adam-Veleni and Koukouvou 2012; Shapland and Stefani 2017; Andreou and Efkleidou 2018).

When the Army of the Orient, initially comprising British and French forces, arrived in Thessaloniki in late 1915, its soldiers began to dig defensive trenches to defend the city (Figure 15). This resulted in, among other finds, the discovery of an Early Neolithic site at Aivatli (Lete) and the identification of a nearby prehistoric mound (Gardner and Casson 1919: 12–15; Dimoula 2017). Both British and French archaeologists were serving in the army, and they made an agreement with the Ephorate that they should gather finds in Thessaloniki. The first curator of the British Salonika Force Museum was Ernest Gardner, who had been Director of the British School at Athens. When the frontline moved north in 1916, Gardner and others began to explore prehistoric sites in the area, including Toumba Thessaloniki, but they generally only collected sherds or dug small exploratory trenches (Cooksey *et al.* 1919; Gardner and Casson 1919). One important site discovered at this time was Dikili Tash, which was only fully excavated after the Second World War (Welch 1919). By contrast the lead French archaeologist Léon Rey conducted systematic excavations at various sites, including the prehistoric mound of Gona. Immediately after the war he published a monograph which put the excavation results in a wider geographical context and also included stratified pottery for the first time (Rey 1919). By the time the troops departed in 1919,

Figure 15 Photograph of British soldiers digging at Aivatli (Lete).
© IWM (Q 13729).

the region of Macedonia had been thoroughly surveyed as a result of military activity and many more prehistoric sites reported.

British involvement in Macedonia continued after the War. Stanley Casson, one of the curators of the British Salonika Force Museum, returned to Macedonia in 1921 in order to explore the mound at Chauchitza, a former British Army camp where Iron Age graves had been discovered. Some of the workers he employed were refugees from the Caucasus (Casson 1925a: 4). Casson was keen to establish the stratification of the mound, which went back to the Bronze Age. He went on to dig another mound at Kilindir with successive Bronze Age and Iron Age levels (Casson 1926: 127–32). His intention was to produce scientific accounts of the different strata, which he felt that Rey's work had lacked. At the same time he drew on nineteenth-century ideas to explain the strata, which at both sites were characterised by a burnt destruction layer at the end of the Bronze Age. This he attributed to the Dorian invasion, while he described the Bronze Age of Chauchitza as a *terramare* culture, invoking Herodotus and the Swiss lake dwellers (Casson 1925b). His experiences of the First World War also informed his thinking since fear of a northern invasion was the reason for the Macedonian Front in the first place (Casson 1921).

Another British archaeologist who first visited Macedonia as a soldier, Walter Heurtley, worked with Casson and went on to excavate a number of other sites using the same principles (Figure 16). As with excavations of tumuli elsewhere in the Aegean, this allowed him to refine the existing pottery chronology. He summarised these excavations in the important publication *Prehistoric Macedonia*, with an associated pottery typology divided into Early, Middle and Late Bronze Age (Heurtley 1939). The Late Bronze Age ceramics included Mycenaean pottery, largely locally made, alongside the handmade burnished wares which characterised the Macedonian Bronze Age. Heurtley's book was an explicit attempt to integrate the archaeology of Macedonia into the Aegean Bronze Age. Nevertheless its study remained largely distinct, its material culture and sites often regarded as less sophisticated than the Mycenaean Greece of the south (Fotiadis 2001; Kotsakis 2017).

Other parts of mainland northern Greece received less archaeological attention until much later. Nineteenth-century travellers, particularly Colonel Leake and Christopher Wordsworth, surveyed Epirus, with a particular interest in finding the classical site of Dodona. Wordsworth did identify the site and later excavations by Dimitrios Evangelidis from 1929 uncovered Bronze Age layers. Other Bronze Age sites were identified by Nicholas Hammond in the 1930s, but his publication and excavations only happened after the Second World War (Tartaron 2004: 18–19). Hammond spent some of the War in the same area, as a British army liaison officer working with local resistance groups. Bronze Age Thrace was also neglected,

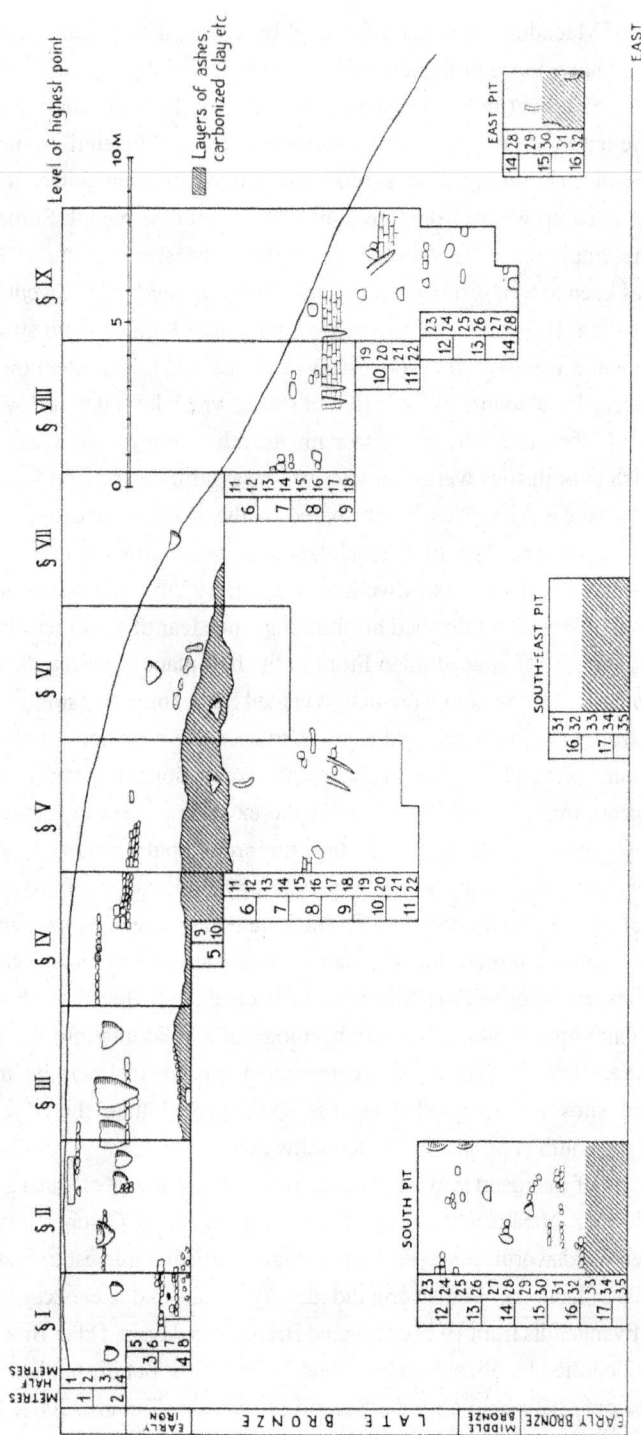

Figure 16 Section drawing of the mound of Vardarophtsa (Heurtley 1939: fig. 37).

although the Ephor of Macedonia Eustratios Pelekides did explore the site of Paradimi in the 1920s (Andreou *et al.* 2001: 313–4).

Major excavations by the Foreign Schools did take place on the islands of the north Aegean. These were mainly in search of classical antiquities, as with French excavations at Thasos and Samothrace. Italian excavations on Lemnos turned to Poliochni in the 1930s, where a major Neolithic and Early Bronze Age site was excavated. The lead archaeologist, Alessandro Della Seta, was interested in the island's traditional connections with the Tyrrhenians/Etruscans (Bernabò Brea 1964; Cultraro 2006). Important finds included an Early Bronze Age public building dubbed the 'Boulouterion' and a hoard of gold jewellery from the same period. Winifred Lamb, a British archaeologist who had worked with Wace and Heurtley, initiated excavations at Thermi on Lesbos in 1929, uncovering an Early Bronze Age settlement (Lamb 1936). Poliochni and Thermi both showed strong similarities with Troy, resulting in a better understanding of the north-east Aegean in the Early Bronze Age. This provided an alternative, regional, context for the 'Priam's Treasure' and 'Priam's Palace' of Troy II instead of the ill-fitting Homeric framework.

5.8 Crete

Crete joined the Greek War of Independence but remained part of the Ottoman Empire. During the nineteenth century, political unrest and violence between the island's Christian and Muslim populations culminated in the Halepa Pact of 1878, which gave more autonomy to the Cretans. It allowed for the establishment of a Society for the Promotion of Education (Σύλλογος Φιλεκπαιδευτικός) in various places, with Minos Kalokairinos a founder member of the Heraklion Syllogos (Kopaka 2015: 143). In 1883, under its new president, Iosif Hatzidakis, it was responsible for the establishment of a collection of antiquities which became the nucleus of Heraklion Archaeological Museum (Hatzidakis 1931; Carabott 2006: 46; Mandalaki 2023). The Heraklion Syllogos sought to prevent new excavations while Crete was still under Ottoman control, and subject to its antiquities laws. In 1898 further rioting led to the 'Great Powers' taking control of the island and installing Prince George of Greece as the governor of an independent Cretan State, albeit still formally part of the Ottoman Empire. The Cretan State passed its own antiquities law in 1899, drafted by Hatzidakis, establishing a museum and two Ephors (Carabott 2006: 47). Foreign excavations were permitted, following lobbying from excavators including Sir Arthur Evans (Brown 2001: 269–304). A further law was passed in 1903 allowing the export of finds from excavations deemed surplus to Cretan museums (Panagiotaki 2004). These measures largely aligned Crete with

Greece. Following further unrest Crete eventually became part of Greece in 1913 under the terms of the Treaty of London, signed at the conclusion of the First Balkan War.

Although the political situation on Crete made excavations difficult until the twentieth century, the search for the location of the mythical Labyrinth goes back much further. Like Troy, the Greek and Roman city of Knossos celebrated its mythical past, but ancient authors including Pliny the Elder suggested that no remains of the Labyrinth survived there.[17] This meant that travellers to Crete from the fifteenth century looked elsewhere, and an underground quarry near the Roman city of Gortyn in the south became a prime candidate (Kotsonas 2018). The Florentine cleric Cristoforo Buondelmonti, who first visited Crete in 1415, identified the Palace of King Minos at Gortyn. His map of the island also showed the Labyrinth near Gortyn rather than at Knossos. The location of Knossos had not been forgotten and coins helped confirm this was the correct site. The debate continued into the nineteenth century. Robert Pashley visited Knossos in 1834, but like many travellers before him, he was disappointed by the ruins he saw. He illustrated coins of Knossos with the Labyrinth design but decided that they 'represent not a material edifice, but a work of the imagination' (Pashley 1837: 208–9). Soon after, Captain Thomas Spratt visited Crete as part of a British naval mission to map the Aegean (Spratt 1865). His map marked Knossos and many other ancient sites, some of which like Phaistos turned out to be Bronze Age in date, but showed the Labyrinth near Gortyn.

The search for the mythical Labyrinth is significant because it provides the context for the excavations at Knossos undertaken by Minos Kalokairinos in 1878. He was aware of Schliemann's discoveries at other Homeric sites and, following the signing of the Halepa Pact, decided to exercise his freedom to dig at Knossos until fellow members of the Syllogos forced him to stop. He uncovered several areas of a building which he identified as the Palace of King Minos although he located the Labyrinth in a Roman quarry nearby, no doubt because of the tradition around the quarry at Gortyn. Kalokairinos did not publish his results at the time but did send several pithoi from the storage magazines at Knossos to museums including the Louvre and the British Museum (Kopaka 2015). This aroused interest in the site and a stream of visitors came to see the excavations over the next few years, including Bernard Hassoullier, who published some of the Mycenaean sherds and William Stillman, who identified the building as the Labyrinth (Hassoullier 1880; Stillman 1881). Some of the visitors tried to establish the rights to excavate including Heinrich Schliemann, André Joubin for the French School at Athens

---

[17] Pliny Natural History 36.19.

and, in 1894, Arthur Evans (Brown 1986; Driessen 2001). Whereas Joubin was mistrusted in Crete because he had tried to gain permission from Constantinople, Evans established good relations with Hatzidakis. Hatzidakis helped Evans to buy a share in the land which later enabled him to purchase the remainder of the site and start excavations. Both Schliemann and Evans were wealthy men who could afford to buy the site but Schliemann's business experience meant that he had walked away from negotiations when he failed to secure what he thought was a fair price.

Although it was difficult to secure excavation permits on Crete until after the 1899 antiquities law was passed, archaeological exploration of the island had begun before Cretan Independence. Federico Halbherr, an Italian classical archaeologist travelled round Crete in search of inscriptions but also excavated at a number of sites including Gortyn and the Idaean Cave. In 1886 he and Hatzidakis undertook a small excavation in Psychro Cave on the Lasithi Plateau following the discovery of a bronze bull figurine there by a local shepherd a few years earlier. They found a few more bronze objects which entered the collection of the Syllogos, and in his report Halbherr compared the objects to recent Mycenaean finds (Halbherr and Orsi 1888). Halbherr also undertook work on behalf of the Archaeological Institute of America in 1894, including the excavation of postpalatial tombs (Halbherr 1901). As part of the same expedition Antonio Taramelli dug at the prehistoric site of Miamou, explored the Kamares Cave, where early pottery had been discovered the year before, and dug a trench at Phaistos where he found more of the same Kamares pottery (Taramelli 1897, 1901a, 1901b). One of the reasons for his interest in Phaistos was the Ayios Onouphrios deposit which had been discovered in 1887 and the contents removed to the Syllogos museum. This contained handmade pottery, stone vessels, seals and marble figurines resembling those already known from the Cyclades. It was first published by Arthur Evans (1895: 56, 105–36), who realised its significance as providing links with the Cycladic or 'Amorgan' period, as he called it.

Arthur Evans' first trip to Crete was in 1894. His research was intertwined with his collection of antiquities for the Ashmolean Museum: he had gone to Crete in order to find inscribed prehistoric objects, having recognised an early writing system on Cretan sealstones he had bought in Athens in 1893 (Evans 1895; Galanakis 2014). Almost immediately he visited Knossos with Kalokairinos, where he was interested in the inscribed masons' marks on the walls. Evans also visited the Syllogos collection in Heraklion to study objects there and started to purchase antiquities from collectors, including objects from Knossos and Psychro. He visited Psychro Cave in the following years to buy antiquities directly from the villagers, who continued to dig there (Brown 2001:

356) (Figure 17). At Psychro Evans purchased part of a stone offering table inscribed with Linear A and initiated an excavation to find other fragments of it (Evans 1897: 350–61). On his travels around the island he bought hundreds more antiquities, including further inscribed sealstones, and also recorded the locations of prehistoric remains. Like other archaeologists he would offer to buy antiquities in the villages he passed through and enquire where they came from, building up a detailed picture of the archaeological landscape. In these early publications Evans had already started to use the term 'Minoan' to describe Crete, following in the footsteps of earlier German scholars such as Karl Hoeck. He also acknowledged the contributions of figures such as Kalokairinos and Halbherr but his later writings tended to obscure the debt his work owed to other scholars (Karadimas 2015).

Figure 17 Photograph of local villagers at Psychro Cave with John Myres, 1895. Arthur Evans (not pictured) accompanied Myres. Myres Archive 2153. © Ashmolean Museum, University of Oxford.

As a result of these archaeological surveys, promising sites had already been located by 1900, and so when Cretan Independence came the archaeologists of different nationalities agreed between themselves where they should dig and then sought permits from the Cretan authorities. An Italian team started excavations at Phaistos, where Taramelli had dug previously. The French gave up their claim to Knossos and focussed on Lato (Goulas), an apparently promising prehistoric site which Evans had wanted to dig himself, but which turned out to be hellenistic. Other British archaeologists headed for east Crete to explore sites where Evans had located remains and bought Bronze Age antiquities. These included Zakros, Petras and Palaikastro (Hogarth 1901; Bosanquet 1902a, 1902b). The British excavators failed to find palaces at the first two sites, which were later discovered by Greek archaeologists after the Second World War. They instead focussed their attention on Palaikastro which is still being excavated by British teams, who have yet to find a palace. Evans also gave advice to an American archaeologist, Harriet Boyd Hawes, on promising sites in the area of the Bay of Mirabello. There she excavated several important Bronze Age sites from 1900 onwards, namely Vronda, Vasiliki and Gournia (Hawes 1908). At Gournia she uncovered a complete Bronze Age town with a central palatial building. These excavations set the pattern for the work of the Foreign Schools on Crete, both by establishing areas of influence and by focussing on major palatial settlements.

Evans' excavation at Knossos achieved much greater international prominence than those at other sites. Some of the finds were spectacular: in the first season of excavation he and his team uncovered a room with a stone seat that they came to identify as the Throne Room of King Minos, helping to prove in his mind that this was indeed a palace (Figure 18). There were also colourful frescoes on the walls, including scenes of bulls and gatherings of people. He embraced the mythical connections of the site and tried to demonstrate that the building was both the Palace of Minos, as he came to call it, and the Labyrinth. Among the evidence he put forward was the double-axe sign carved in the walls, which he had first seen in the area Kalokairinos had exposed. Using a questionable etymology for 'Labyrinth' he connected this with the later Carian 'labrys' double-axe sign. As he noted in his 1900 report, 'the appearance of this *labrys* symbol on the great prehistoric building of Knossos, coupled with many other points in the discoveries, such as the great bulls, the harem-scenes, the long corridors and blind-ending magazines, can hardly leave any remaining doubt that we have here the original of the traditional Labyrinth' (Evans 1900: 33). Like Schliemann he also publicised his discoveries through letters to *The Times* and two exhibitions in London. The rediscovery of the Labyrinth was a compelling story, and Kalokairinos' role in it was downplayed. The discovery of Linear B tablets too offered the tantalising hope of new historical or literary texts.

Figure 18 Workers excavating the Throne Room at Knossos, 1900. Sir Arthur Evans Archive AJE/3/1/12/22/1. © Ashmolean Museum, University of Oxford.

The excavation of the palace at Knossos took place initially over six seasons, from 1900 to 1905, starting with the West Wing where Kalokairinos had dug before. Excavation of the surrounding area continued alongside further work in the palace until 1931 (Hood and Taylor 1981: 1–11). When the palace had been fully uncovered, Evans and Mackenzie started to explore underground cists, resulting in the discovery in 1903 of the Snake Goddesses and other faience finds in the 'Temple Repositories'. Evocative names like this, which Evans gave to various spaces, helped to embed the idea that this was a palace and temple, with separate male and female spaces (the 'King's Megaron' and 'Queen's Megaron') and even connections to later Greek architecture (the 'South Propylaeum'). Some of these were derived from names Schliemann and Dörpfeld had applied to the palace at Tiryns. They were also taken up by excavators at Phaistos, Halbherr and Luigi Pernier, who uncovered a very similar building from 1900 to 1909 (Pernier 1935; Pernier and Banti 1951; La Rosa 2012b). They too identified men's and women's megara, resulting in a homogenised view of these buildings. As at Knossos, further seasons took place in the 1920s and 1930s in order to understand the pottery and stratigraphy better, alongside restorations. At both sites restorations were needed to consolidate the architectural remains and protect vulnerable areas but Evans took these one stage further by using reinforced concrete to bring his vision of the

Palace of Minos to life, at the same time as supporting some of his theories about the site (Hitchcock and Koudounaris 2002; Papadopoulos 2005; Gere 2009).

The mortuary archaeology of prehistoric Crete developed alongside these palatial excavations. Although David Hogarth had prospected the area around the palace at Knossos for tombs in 1900, he did not find what he was looking for and moved on to excavate the Psychro Cave instead, blasting his way into the lower cave with dynamite (Hogarth 1900a, 1900b). Evans and Mackenzie began to look for tombs further up the Knossos valley from 1904, soon finding a Late Bronze Age cemetery at Zafer Papoura. They moved on to the 'Royal Tomb' at Isopata which had already been emptied and quarried for stone by the landowner (Evans 1906b). Further tombs were found by a local vineyard owner soon after and excavated by Evans and Mackenzie from 1910. Evans' final excavation at Knossos, in 1931, was the 'Temple Tomb', which he believed was a cenotaph for King Minos (Evans 1935: 962–87). Tombs were also discovered at Ayia Triada, where Halbherr had started to excavate in 1902 in search of the necropolis of Phaistos (La Rosa 2012b). The remains turned out to be a building they termed a 'Villa' because it had a different ground plan from the palaces. Finds included a number of carved stone vessels: the 'Harvester Vase', the 'Chieftain Cup' and the 'Boxer Rhyton' (Figure 19).[18] The following year they did find a Mycenaean tomb which contained a sarcophagus decorated with painted plaster scenes showing cult activity, most likely associated with the burial (Long 1974).[19]

The Early Minoan tombs of Crete started to be excavated at a similar time. Stephanos Xanthoudides, the director of Heraklion Museum and Ephor of Crete, began to excavate tombs in the Mesara in 1904 as a result of finds from Koumasa being handed in to the museum. There he found four stone tombs, three of which were circular. A similar circular tomb at Ayia Triada had been excavated by Federico Halbherr that year, and they came to be known as tholoi like the similar Mycenaean tombs. Xanthoudides carried on excavating at various sites, including Platanos and Marathokephalo until 1918, rapidly publishing his finds (Xanthoudides 1924) (Figure 20). Although many were already known locally – the tomb at Kalathiana had first been dug in 1854 – he found intact deposits at many of them containing impressive finds, including jewellery and bronze weapons, as well as more Cycladic figurines, as at Ayios Onouphrios. In east Crete other Prepalatial burials had come to light at Palaikastro (Bosanquet 1902a), and also the Early Minoan cemeteries at Mochlos. These were excavated in 1907–8 by the American Richard Seager,

---

[18] Heraklion Archaeological Museum Λ 184 (Harvester Vase), Λ 341 (Chieftain Cup), Λ 342, 498, 676 (Boxer Rhyton).
[19] Heraklion Archaeological Museum Λ 396.

Figure 19 Photograph of plaster replicas of relief stone vessels from Ayia Triada. Sir Arthur Evans Archive. © Ashmolean Museum, University of Oxford.

who found rich tombs containing gold jewellery and stone vessels (Seager 1912). Seager excavated a number of other sites in the area, including the Minoan town on the island of Pseira (Seager 1910). Exploration of tombs continued into the Second World War. Among the *Kunstschutz* excavations on Crete was a tholos tomb at Apesokari, whose finds were deposited in Heraklion Museum (Flouda 2017).

Iosif Hatzidakis also began excavating Minoan sites, including Tylissos, from 1909 until 1913 (Hatzidakis 1921). He then turned his attention to Mallia, where he started to uncover a palace in 1915, allowing French excavators to continue work in the 1920s (Chapouthier 1928; Chapouthier and Joly 1936; Pelon *et al.* 1980). There they also started to explore the nearby tombs, including the Chryssolakkos necropolis, where the famous gold bee pendant

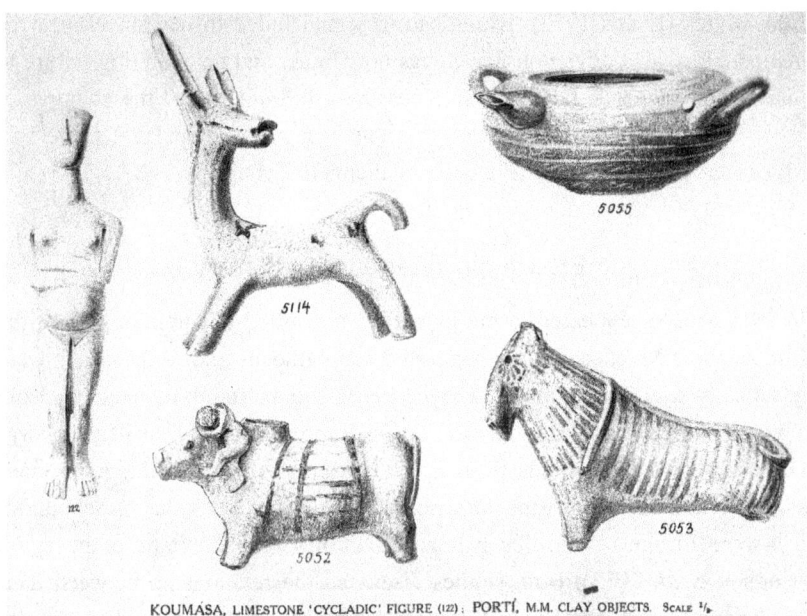

Figure 20 Drawings of finds from Koumasa and Porti (Xanthoudides 1924: pl. VII).

was found (Demargne 1930).[20] Xanthoudides' successor as Ephor and director of Heraklion Museum, Spyridon Marinatos, also started work at various sites in the 1930s, including Arkalochori Cave, where a hoard of Bronze Age metalwork had been discovered. He also excavated the villa at Amnisos, finding wall paintings preserved in a destruction layer which he linked with the eruption of the Thera volcano (Marinatos 1939: 433–4). This prompted his theory that Minoan civilisation collapsed following a tsunami, and also led him to renew the excavations at Thera after the Second World War.

Excavations at various sites revealed further examples of the Cretan scripts that Evans had first identified. Clay tablets bearing Cretan Hieroglyphic were found at Knossos and Mallia, while Linear A tablets were found at Ayia Triada, Palaikastro and Zakros. The most intriguing clay document, the Phaistos Disc, was discovered in 1908 in a building next to the palace. Unlike other clay documents the signs were stamped rather than incised, and it remains unique. Evans continued to be at the forefront of studying these Cretan scripts, publishing inscribed seals and documents, including the Phaistos Disc, in the first volume of *Scripta Minoa* (Evans 1909). The second volume, focussing on the Linear B tablets, was only published after his death and was brought to press by

---

[20] Heraklion Archaeological Museum X-A 559.

John Myres (Evans 1952). Evans had tried and failed to decipher Linear B, hampered by his conviction that it was not Greek, and his resulting failure to publish the Linear B tablets from Knossos in full obstructed the attempts of others. The decipherment showed that the final phase of palatial Crete was Mycenaean, which would have been anathema to Evans.

6 Broadening Aegean Prehistory

In 2017 a paper appeared in the journal *Nature* titled 'Genetic origins of the Minoans and Mycenaeans'. It suggested that Minoans and Mycenaeans were genetically similar, although the Mycenaeans had an additional ancestry from a region to the north (Lazaridis *et al.* 2017). Representative of the Minoans was DNA extracted from skulls from Bronze Age burials in Lasithi. A previous study on the same skulls used mitochondrial DNA to suggest that these individuals were 'European' and closely related to the modern inhabitants of the region (Hughey *et al.* 2013). Both studies discussed the relationship between their results and the spread of Indo-European languages. A century earlier, Charles Henry Hawes had come to the same conclusion using the then cutting-edge scientific technique of craniometry, resulting in the idea that the 'old Minoan type' was to be found predominantly in Lasithi and other mountainous areas of Crete (Hawes and Hawes 1911: 25). Like many others of his time, he was interested in the relationship between race, language and invasions from the north, except he used the term 'Aryan' rather than 'Indo-European'. On one level it is not surprising that questions relating to origins and identity continue to be asked, or that scientific techniques for answering them improve over time. The same could be said of the history of prehistoric Aegean archaeology in general. From this point of view the history of the discipline charts the growth of knowledge and improvement of techniques for answering fundamental questions about the origins of past and present Aegean populations.

One of the reasons for exploring disciplinary history, however, is to show how these questions and terms can be located in particular historical conditions. Minoans and Mycenaeans, like Pelasgians and Carians before them, are terms which archaeologists applied to assemblages of objects at a certain time to make sense of them by equating them with a people or culture. By tracing how these terms change, and the associated debates about language and race, these terms themselves become historical artefacts rather than neutral descriptions. Ancient DNA is a powerful tool for understanding past populations, but using it to identify 'Minoans', Mycenaeans' or 'Europeans' simply perpetuates a nineteenth-century understanding of archaeological cultures as akin to modern nationalities (Greenberg and Hamilakis 2022: 139–48). There have been attempts to move away from these constricting terms. Colin Renfrew, an early advocate of processual archaeology in Aegean Prehistory, proposed terms such as 'Korakou culture' or 'Grotta-Pelos culture' to define more regional assemblages (Renfrew 1972). More recent debates about Minoanisation and Mycenaeanisation have also tended to explore the relationship between stylistic groups of objects and people rather than assuming that they equate one another (Broodbank 2004; Gorogianni et al. 2016). Understanding the origin of these terms and historicising them is an important way to rethink the stories archaeologists tell about the Bronze Age.

Another reason for retelling disciplinary history is to understand the gaps. Traditional archaeological histories have relied on archaeologists' accounts, but these often create a divide between the archaeologist as discoverer and the local inhabitants as treasure hunters or looters. The call for 'indigenous archaeologies' seeks to record and validate other types of material engagement with the traces of the past, such as worship or reusing spolia as alternative types of archaeological activities (Hamilakis 2011). Although it is useful to consider local perspectives, this can simplify a more complex situation. Government officials, for instance, sometimes played another role which Varouchakis (2017: 44) terms the 'collaborator class' since they helped impose a legal framework which favoured archaeologists over locals, so that archaeology became legalised digging rather than illegal looting. Although archaeological excavation and recording techniques did become more sophisticated over time, the only criterion which can be used to define archaeological excavation in the Aegean in the period discussed here is that it is recorded and then published. In many cases, whether at Thera, or Amorgos or Psychro, archaeologists simply recorded local excavations. In other cases, such as at Knossos or Troy, the difference between archaeologist and local was simply one of resources to excavate and publish. Minos Kalokairinos and Frank Calvert do appear fleetingly in acknowledgements and footnotes, and their work has been subsequently recognised. But they are the exceptions that help to show that behind every archaeological publication there is a longer history of local knowledge and local participation that is easy to overlook.

A further reason for retelling disciplinary history is to question the accepted narratives. A common trope is the luck of the archaeologist in finding an unlooted tomb or an intact destruction layer containing well-preserved artefacts. What this narrative lacks is the role of the object or site in creating the moment of discovery. Schliemann's discoveries at Mycenae, and to a lesser extent Troy, are famous because he uncovered objects which still attract crowds in museums. In the early twentieth century, many European museums bought replicas of objects such as the Mask of Agamemnon, the Vapheio Cups, the Harvester Vase and the Snake Goddesses. These charismatic objects, and their reproduction in print or through replication, helped to engage a broader public because of their strangeness, beauty or elaborate crafting. The same can be said of inscribed objects like Linear B tablets or the Phaistos Disc, which create a sense of mystery and an opportunity for decipherment, and even conspiracy theories about their authenticity. At the moment of discovery an object such as the Mask of Agamemnon becomes entangled in a new set of relations as it is reported, illustrated, described and even replicated. Objects, and not just archaeologists, can have biographies and become famous.

One of the challenges of a critical disciplinary history is that sites and objects are already embedded in public narratives. The use of sites like Troy, Knossos or Mycenae for reinforcing national identity is well-known (Andreou 2005; Voutsaki 2017). Historicising concepts such as Minoan and Mycenaean can be perceived as a threat to local identities or the tourist industry, for which they are unproblematic terms. However hard archaeologists try to reflect critically on their discipline, television programmes and exhibitions will continue to focus on the famous archaeologists and the well-known sites or objects. Even so, as the scope of decolonisation broadens, there is an opportunity to tell more inclusive stories that will appeal to a public already fascinated by the romance of archaeology.

References

Adam-Veleni, P. and Koukouvou, A., eds. (2012). *Αρχαιολογία στα μετόπισθεν. Στη Θεσσαλονίκη των ταραγμένων χρόνων 1912–1922/Archaeology behind Battle Lines. In Thessaloniki of the Turbulent Years 1912–1922*. Thessaloniki: Archaeological Museum of Thessaloniki.

Allen, S. H. (1999). *Finding the Walls of Troy: Frank Calvert and Heinrich Schliemann at Hisarlik*. Berkeley: University of California Press.

Allsebrook, M. (1992). *Born to Rebel: The Life of Harriet Boyd Hawes*. Oxford: Oxbow Books.

Andreou, S. (2005). The landscapes of modern Greek Aegean Prehistory. In J. Cherry, D. Margomenou and L. E. Talalay, eds., *Prehistorians Round the Pond: Reflections on Aegean Prehistory as a Discipline*. Ann Arbor: Kelsey Museum of Archaeology, pp. 73–92.

Andreou, S. and Efkleidou, K. (2018). *Η αρχαιολογία στη γραμμή του πυρός: αρχαιότητες και αρχαιολογική έρευνα στη Μακεδονία του Α' Παγκοσμίου Πολέμου*. Thessaloniki: University Studio Press.

Andreou, S., Fotiadis, M. and Kotsakis, K. (2001). Review of Aegean Prehistory V: The Neolithic and Bronze Age of northern Greece. In T. Cullen ed., *Aegean Prehistory: A Review*. Boston: Archaeological Institute of America, pp. 537–597.

Aravantinos, V. (2006). Le cas de Thèbes (Béotie): Mythe, idéologie et recherche au debut du XXe siècle. In P. Darcque, M. Fotiadis and O. Polychronopoulou, eds., *Mythos: la préhistoire égéenne du XIXe au XXIe siècle après J.-C*. Athens: École Française d'Athènes, pp. 165–174.

Arnott, R. (1990). Early Cycladic objects from Ios formerly in the Finlay collection. *Annual of the British School at Athens* 85: 1–14. https://doi.org/10.1017/S0068245400015525.

Atkinson, T. D., Bosanquet, R. C., Edgar, C. C., et al. (1904). *Excavations at Phylakopi in Melos*. London: Society for the Promotion of Hellenic Studies.

Avgouli, M. (1994). The first Greek museums and national identity. In F. E. S. Kaplan, ed., *Museums and the Making of 'Ourselves': The Role of the Objects in National Identity*. London: Leicester University Press, pp. 246–265.

Bahrani, Z., Çelik, Z. and Eldem, E. (2011). Introduction: Archaeology and empire. In Z. Bahrani, Z. Çelik and E. Eldem, eds., *Scramble for the Past: A Story of Archaeology in the Ottoman Empire, 1753–1914*. Istanbul: SALT, pp. 13–43.

Baker, A. (2019). *Troy on Display: Scepticism and Wonder at Schliemann's First Exhibition*. London: Bloomsbury.

Barchard, D. (2006). The fearless and self-reliant servant: The life and career of Sir Alfred Biliotti (1833–1915), an Italian Levantine in British service. *Studi Micenei ed Egeo-Anatolici* 48: 5–53.

Beaton, R. (2019). *Greece: Biography of a Modern Nation*. London: Allen Lane.

Becker, M. and Betancourt, P. P. (1997). *Richard Berry Seager: Pioneer Archaeologist and Proper Gentleman*. Philadelphia: UPenn Museum of Archaeology.

Beckman, G., Bryce, T. and Cline, E. (2011). *The Ahhiyawa Texts*. Leiden: Brill.

Belon, P. (1555). *Les observations de plusieurs singularitez & choses memorables, trouvées en Grece, Asie, Iudée, Egypte, Arabie, & autres pays estranges, redigées en trois liures*. Paris: Chez Guillaume Cauellet.

Bent, J. T. (1885). *The Cyclades, or, Life Among the Insular Greeks*. London: Longmans, Green and Co.

Benton, S. (1935). Excavations in Ithaca, III. *Annual of the British School at Athens* 35: 45–73. https://doi.org/10.1017/S0068245400007383.

Benzi, M. (2009). Le prime tombe micenee scoperte da archeologi italiani a Rodi. In A. M. Jasink and L. Bombardieri, eds., *Le collezioni egee del Museo Archeologico Nazionale di Firenze*. Florence: Firenze University Press, pp. 372–378.

Bernabò Brea, L. (1964). *Poliochni, città preistorica nell'isola di Lemnos, I*. Roma: 'L'Erma' di Bretschneider.

Blegen, C. W. (1921). *Korakou: A Prehistoric Settlement near Corinth*. Boston: American School of Classical Studies at Athens.

Blegen, C. W. (1928). *Zygouries: A Prehistoric Settlement in the Valley of Cleonae*. Cambridge, MA: Harvard University Press.

Blegen, C. W. (1937). *Prosymna: The Helladic Settlement Preceding the Argive Heraeum*. Cambridge: Cambridge University Press.

Blegen, C. W. and Rawson, M. (1966). *The Palace of Nestor at Pylos in Western Messenia, I. The Buildings and their Contents*. Princeton: Princeton University Press.

Blegen, C. W., Angel, J. L., Caskey, J. L., Rawson, M. and Boulter, C. G. (1950). *Troy: General Introduction. The First and Second Settlements*. Princeton: Princeton University Press.

Blegen, C. W., Caskey, J. L. and Rawson, M. (1953). *Troy: The Sixth Settlement*. Princeton: Princeton University Press.

Blouet, A. (1833). *Expedition scientifique de Morée ordonnée par le Gouvernement Français; Architecture, Sculptures, Inscriptions et Vues du Péloponèse, des Cyclades et de l'Attique, II*. Paris: Firmin Didot Frères.

Bosanquet, R. C. (1897). Notes from the Cyclades. *Annual of the British School at Athens* 3: 52–70. https://doi.org/10.1017/S0068245400000757.

Bosanquet, R. C. (1902a). Excavations at Palaikastro. I. *Annual of the British School at Athens* 8: 286–316. https://doi.org/10.1017/S0068245400001489.

Bosanquet, R. C. (1902b). Excavations at Petras. *Annual of the British School at Athens* 8: 282–285. https://doi.org/10.1017/S0068245400001477.

Bosanquet, R. C., Dawkins, R. M., Tod, M. N., Duckworth, W. L. H., and Myres, J. L. (1903). Excavations at Palaikastro. II. *Annual of the British School at Athens* 9: 274–387.

Brodbeck-Jucker, S. (1986). *Mykenische Funde von Kephallenia im Archäologischen Museum Neuchâtel*. Rome: Giorgio Bretschneider.

Brongniart, A. and Riocreux, D. (1845). *Description méthodique du musée céramique de la manufacture royale de porcelaine de Sèvres*. Paris: Leleux.

Broodbank, C. (2004). Minoanisation. *The Cambridge Classical Journal* 50: 46–91. https://doi.org/10.1017/S006867350000105X.

Brown, A. (1986). 'I propose to begin at Gnossos': John Myres's visit to Crete in 1893. *Annual of the British School at Athens* 81: 37–44. https://doi.org/10.1017/S0068245400020074.

Brown, A. (2001). *Arthur Evans's Travels in Crete, 1894–1899*. Oxford: Archaeopress.

Bulle, H. (1907). *Orchomenos, I, Die älteren Ansiedelungsschichten*. Munich: Verlag der k. B. Akademie der Wissenschaften.

Burgon, T. (1847). An attempt to point out the vases of Greece proper which belong to the Heroic and Homeric Ages. *Transactions of the Royal Society of Literature* 2: 258–296.

Calder, W. M. (1972). Schliemann on Schliemann: A study in the use of sources. *Greek, Roman and Byzantine Studies* 13: 335–353.

Calder, W. M. and Traill, D. A. (1986). *Myth, Scandal, and History: The Heinrich Schliemann Controversy and a First Edition of the Mycenaean Diary*. Detroit: Wayne State University Press.

Carabott, P. (2006). A country in a 'state of destitution' labouring under an 'unfortunate regime': Crete at the turn of the 20th century (1898–1906). In Y. Hamilakis and N. Momigliano, eds., *Archaeology and European Modernity: Producing and Consuming the 'Minoans'*. Padua: Bottega d'Erasmo, pp. 39–53.

Casson, S. (1921). The Dorian Invasion reviewed in the light of some new evidence. *The Antiquaries Journal* 1(3): 199–221. https://doi.org/10.1017/S0003581500002249.

Casson, S. (1925a). Excavations in Macedonia. II. *Annual of the British School at Athens* 26: 1–29. https://doi.org/10.1017/S0068245400010522.

Casson, S. (1925b). The Bronze Age in Macedonia. *Archaeologia* 74: 73–88.

Casson, S. (1926). *Macedonia, Thrace and Illyria: Their Relations to Greece from the Earliest Times Down to the Time of Philip Son of Amyntas*. Oxford: Oxford University Press.

Casson, S. (1939). *The Discovery of Man: The Story of the Inquiry into Human Origins*. London: Hamish Hamilton.

Chadwick, J. (1958). *The Decipherment of Linear B*. Cambridge: Cambridge University Press.

Chapouthier, F. (1928). *Fouilles exécutées à Mallia. Premier rapport* (1922–1924). Paris: Geuthner.

Chapouthier, F. and Joly, R. (1936). *Fouilles exécutées à Mallia. Deuxième rapport. Exploration du Palais* (1925–1926). Paris: Geuthner.

Childe, V. G. (1926). *The Aryans: A Study of Indo-European Origins*. London: Kegan Paul, Trench, Trübner.

Childe, V. G. (1957). *The Dawn of European Civilization*. 6th ed. London: Routledge & Kegan Paul.

Choiseul-Gouffier, M. G. A. F. (1809). *Voyage pittoresque de la Grèce, II*. Paris: Blaise.

Clarke, E. D. (1814). *Travels in Various Countries of Europe, Asia, and Africa, II,2. Greece, Egypt, and the Holy Land*. London: Cadell and Davies.

Clogg, R. (2017). Foreign archaeologists in Greece in time of war. In A. J. Shapland and E. Stefani, eds., *Archaeology behind the Battle Lines: The Macedonian Campaign (1915–1919) and its Legacy*. London: Routledge, pp. 40–57.

Cook, J. M. (1973). *The Troad: An Archaeological and Topographical Study*. Oxford: Clarendon Press.

Cook, R. M. (1955). Thucydides as archaeologist. *Annual of the British School at Athens* 50: 266–270. https://doi.org/10.1017/S0068245400018682.

Cooksey, W., Woodward, A. M. and Casson, S. (1919). Macedonia. IV. Mounds and other ancient sites in the region of Salonika. *Annual of the British School at Athens* 23: 51–63. https://doi.org/10.1017/S0068245400003695.

Cottrell, L. (1955). *The Bull of Minos*. London: Pan.

Cultraro, M. (2006). Islands out of time: Richness and diversity of prehistoric studies on the Northern Aegean. In P. Darcque, M. Fotiadis and

O. Polychronopoulou, eds., *Mythos: la préhistoire égéenne du XIXe au XXIe siècle après J.-C.* Athens: École Française d'Athènes, pp. 279–290.

D'Agata, A. L. (2010). The many lives of a ruin: History and metahistory of the Palace of Minos at Knossos. In O. Krzyszkowska, ed., *Cretan Offerings: Studies in Honour of Peter Warren.* London: British School at Athens, pp. 57–69.

Daniel, G. (1950). *A Hundred Years of Archaeology.* London: Duckworth.

Davis, J. L. (2015). Blegen and the palace of Nestor: What took so long? In N. Vogeikoff-Brogan, J. L. Davis and V. Florou, eds., *Carl W. Blegen: Personal and Archaeological Narratives.* Atlanta: Lockwood Press, pp. 209–230.

Dawkins, R. M. and Woodward, A. M. (1910). Laconia. I. Excavations at Sparta, 1910. *Annual of the British School at Athens* 16: 1–61. https://doi.org/10.1017/S006824540000160X.

de Ridder, A. (1894). Fouilles de Gha. *Bulletin de Correspondance Hellénique* 18: 271–310.

Demargne, P. (1930). Bijoux Minoens de Mallia. *Bulletin de Correspondance Hellénique* 54: 404–421.

Dimoula, A. (2017). 'In the trenches': Old sites, new finds and the Early Neolithic Period in Macedonia, Greece. In A. J. Shapland and E. Stefani, eds., *Archaeology behind the Battle Lines: The Macedonian Campaign (1915–1919) and its Legacy.* London: Routledge, pp. 281–298.

Dodwell, E. (1819). *A Classical and Topographical Tour through Greece, during the Years 1801, 1805, and 1806, II.* London: Rodwell & Martin.

Dodwell, E. (1834). *Views and Descriptions of Cyclopian, or, Pelasgic Remains, in Greece and Italy.* London: Adolphus Richter.

Dörpfeld, W. (1902). *Troja und Ilion: Ergebnisse der Ausgrabungen in den vorhistorischen und historischen Schichten von Ilion, 1870–1894.* Athens: Beck & Barth.

Dörpfeld, W. and Goessler, P. (1927). *Alt-Ithaka: ein Beitrag zur Homer-Frage, Studien und Ausgrabungen aus der insel Leukas-Ithaka.* München: R. Uhde.

Driessen, J. (2001). La bataille de Cnossos. Kalokairinos, Schliemann et Evans. In M. Lodewijckx, ed., *Belgian Archaeology in a European Setting, I.* Leuven: Leuven University Press, pp. 113–117.

Driessen, J. (2024). Never-never land under attack: Axis war damage to Cretan antiquities. In A. Crisà, ed., *Archaeology, Cultural Heritage and World War II. Italy, Greece, France and Finland as Historical Contexts.* Leiden: Brill, pp. 208–245.

Driessen, J. and Kalantzopoulou, T. (2024). *Taking Home Agamemnon: The Casts of the Lion Gate at Mycenae*. Louvain-la-Neuve: Presses universitaires de Louvain.

Dümmler, F. (1886). Mitteilungen von den griechischen Inseln: I. Reste vorgriechischer Bevölkerung auf den Cykladen. *Mitteilungen des Deutschen Archäologischen Instituts, Athenische Abteilung* 11: 15–46.

Dumont, A. (1867a). La Age de Pierre en Grèce. *Revue Archéologique* 15: 16–19.

Dumont, A. (1867b). La Grèce avant la légende et avant l'histoire. *Revue Archéologique* 16: 141–147.

Dumont, A. and Chaplain, J. (1888). *Céramiques de la Grèce propre*. Paris: Firmin Didot Frères.

Easton, D. F. (1994). Priam's Gold: The full story. *Anatolian Studies* 44: 221–243.

Eldem, E. (2011). From blissful indifference to anguished concern: Ottoman perceptions of antiquities, 1799–1869. In Z. Bahrani, Z. Çelik and E. Eldem, eds., *Scramble for the Past: A Story of Archaeology in the Ottoman Empire, 1753–1914*. Istanbul: SALT, pp. 281–329.

Ellis, H. (1833). *Elgin and Phigaleian Marbles, II*. London: Charles Knight.

Étienne, R., ed. (1996). *L'Espace grec. Cent cinquante ans de fouilles de l'École française d'Athènes*. Paris: Fayard.

Evans, A. J. (1893). A Mykênæan Treasure from Ægina. *Journal of Hellenic Studies* 13: 195–226. https://doi.org/10.2307/623904.

Evans, A. J. (1895). *Cretan Pictographs and Prae-Phoenician Script with an Account of a Sepulchral Deposit at Hagios Onuphrios near Phaestos in its Relation to Primitive Cretan and Aegean Culture*. London: Quaritch.

Evans, A. J. (1897). Further discoveries of Cretan and Aegean script: with Libyan and Proto-Egyptian comparisons. *Journal of Hellenic Studies* 17: 327–395.

Evans, A. J. (1900). Knossos: Summary report of the excavations in 1900: I. The palace. *Annual of the British School at Athens* 6: 3–70. https://doi.org/10.1017/S0068245400001908.

Evans, A. J. (1906a). *Essai de classification des époques de la civilisation minoenne: résumé d'un discours fait au Congrès d'Archéologie à Athènes*. London: Quaritch.

Evans, A. J. (1906b). *The Prehistoric Tombs of Knossos*. London: Quaritch.

Evans, A. J. (1909). *Scripta Minoa, I*. Oxford: Clarendon Press.

Evans, A. J. (1921). *The Palace of Minos at Knossos, I*. London: Macmillan.

Evans, A. J. (1929). *The Shaft Graves and Bee-Hive Tombs of Mycenae and their Interrelation*. London: Macmillan.

Evans, A. J. (1935). *The Palace of Minos at Knossos, IV.* London: Macmillan.
Evans, A. J. (1952). *Scripta Minoa, II.* Oxford: Clarendon Press.
Evans, J. (1943). *Time and Chance: The Story of Arthur Evans and his Forebears.* London: Longmans.
Farnoux, A. (1993). *Cnossos: l'archéologie d'un rêve.* Paris: Gallimard.
Finlay, G. (1869). *Παρατηρήσεις ἐπ τῆς ἐν Ἑλβετίᾳ καὶ Ἑλλάδι Προϊστορικῆς Ἀρχαιολογίας.* Athens: Laconias.
Fitton, J. L. (1995). *The Discovery of the Greek Bronze Age.* London: British Museum Press.
Fitton, J. L., Meeks, N. and Williams, D. (2009). *The Aigina Treasure: Aegean Bronze Age Jewellery and a Mystery Revisited.* London: British Museum Press.
Flouda, G. (2017). Archaeology in the war zone: August Schörgendorfer and the Kunstschutz on Crete during World War II. *Annual of the British School at Athens* 112: 1–37.
Forrer, E. (1924). Vorhomerische Griechen in den Keilschrifttexten von Boghazköi. *Mitteilungen der Deutschen Orient-Gesellschaft* 63: 1–24.
Fotiadis, M. (2001). Imagining Macedonia in prehistory, ca. 1900–1930. *Journal of Mediterranean Archaeology* 14: 115–135. https://doi.org/10.1558/jmea.v14i2.115.
Fotiadis, M. (2016). Aegean Prehistory without Schliemann. *Hesperia* 85: 91–119.
Fotiadis, M. (2017). Are histories of archaeology good to think with? In S. Voutsaki and P. Cartledge, eds., *Ancient Monuments and Modern Identities: A Critical History of Archaeology in 19th and 20th Century Greece.* London: Routledge, pp. 186–198.
Fouqué, F. (1879). *Santorin et ses éruptions.* Paris: G. Masson.
Fox, M. (2013). *The Riddle of the Labyrinth: The Quest to Crack an Ancient Code and the Uncovering of a Lost Civilisation.* London: Profile Books.
Frödin, O. and Persson, A. (1938). *Asine: Results of the Swedish Excavations 1922–1930.* Stockholm: Generalstabens litografiska anstalts förlag.
Furtwängler, A. (1900). *Die antiken Gemmen: Geschichte der Steinschneidekunst im klassischen Altertum.* Leipzig and Berlin: Giesecke & Devrient.
Furtwängler, A. and Loeschcke, G. (1879). *Mykenische Thongefäße.* Berlin: Asher.
Furtwängler, A. and Loeschcke, G. (1886). *Mykenische Vasen.* Berlin: Asher.
Furumark, A. (1941). *The Mycenaean Pottery: Analysis and Classification.* Stockholm: Kungl. Vitterhets Historie och Antikvitets Akademien.

Galanakis, Y. (2011). An unpublished stirrup jar from Athens and the 1871–2 private excavations in the Outer Kerameikos. *Annual of the British School at Athens* 106: 167–200. https://doi.org/10.1017/S0068245411000074.

Galanakis, Y. (2013). Early prehistoric research on Amorgos and the beginnings of Cycladic archaeology. *American Journal of Archaeology* 117(2): 181–205. https://doi.org/10.3764/aja.117.2.0181.

Galanakis, Y. (2014). Arthur Evans and the quest for the 'origins of Mycenaean culture'. In Y. Galanakis, T. Wilkinson and J. Bennet, eds., *AΘYPMATA: Critical Essays on the Archaeology of the Eastern Mediterranean in Honour of E. Susan Sherratt*. Oxford: Archaeopress, pp. 85–98.

Galanakis, Y. (2015). 'Islanders v. Mainlanders', 'the Mycenae Wars', & other short stories. In N. Vogeikoff-Brogan, J. L. Davis and V. Florou, eds., *Carl W. Blegen: Personal and Archaeological Narratives*. Atlanta: Lockwood Press, pp. 99–120.

Gallis, C. (1979). A short chronicle of the Greek archaeological investigations in Thessaly, from 1881 until to the present day In B. Helly, ed., *La Thessalie. Actes de la Table-Ronde, 21–24 juillet 1975, Lyon*. Lyon: Maison de l'Orient, pp. 1–30.

Gardner, E. and Casson, S. (1919). Macedonia. II. Antiquities found in the British zone 1915–1919. *Annual of the British School at Athens* 23: 10–43.

Gardner, P. (1880). Stephani on the Tombs at Mycenae. *Journal of Hellenic Studies* 1: 94–106. https://doi.org/10.2307/623616.

Gazi, A. (2008). 'Artfully classified' and 'appropriately placed': Notes on the display of antiquities in early twentieth-century Greece. In D. Damaskos and D. Plantzos, eds., *A Singular Antiquity: Archaeology and Hellenic Identity in Twentieth-Century Greece*. Athens: Benaki Museum, pp. 67–82.

Gazi, A. (2017). Displaying archaeology: Exhibiting ideology in 19th and early 20th century Greek museums. In S. Voutsaki and P. Cartledge, eds., *Ancient Monuments and Modern Identities: A History of Archaeology in 19th and 20th Century Greece*. London: Routledge, pp. 95–116.

Gell, W. (1804). *The Topography of Troy*. London: Longman & Rees.

Gell, W. (1810). *The Itinerary of Greece: With a Commentary on Pausanias and Strabo and an Account of the Monuments of Antiquity at Present Existing in that Country*. London: T. Payne.

Gere, C. (2006). *The Tomb of Agamemnon*. Cambridge, MA: Harvard University Press.

Gere, C. (2009). *Knossos and the Prophets of Modernism*. Chicago: University of Chicago Press.

Gill, D. W. J. (2011a). Excavating under gunfire: Archaeologists in the Aegean during the First World War. *Public Archaeology* 10: 187–199. https://doi.org/10.1179/175355311X13206765126596.

Gill, D. W. J. (2011b). *Sifting the Soil of Greece: The Early Years of the British School at Athens (1886–1919)*. London: Institute of Classical Studies.

Gill, D. W. J. (2018). *Winifred Lamb: Aegean Prehistorian and Museum Curator*. Oxford: Archaeopress.

Gill, D. W. J. and Chippindale, C. (1993). Material and intellectual consequences of esteem for Cycladic figures. *American Journal of Archaeology* 97(4): 601–659. https://doi.org/10.2307/506716.

Goldman, H. (1931). *Excavations at Eutresis in Boeotia*. Cambridge, MA: Harvard University Press.

Gorogianni, E., Pavúk, P. and Girella, L., eds. (2016). *Beyond Thalassocracies: Understanding Processes of Minoanisation and Mycenaeanisation in the Aegean*. Oxford: Oxbow.

Greenberg, R. and Hamilakis, Y. (2022). *Archaeology, Nation, and Race: Confronting the Past, Decolonizing the Future in Greece and Israel*. Cambridge: Cambridge University Press. https://doi.org/10.1017/9781009160247.

Grote, G. (1846). *History of Greece, I*. London: John Murray.

Grundon, I. (2007). *The Rash Adventurer: A Life of John Pendlebury*. London: Libri.

Gunning, L. P. (2009). *The British Consular Service in the Aegean and the Collection of Antiquities for the British Museum*. Farnham: Ashgate.

Halbherr, F. (1901). Cretan Expedition XI. Three Cretan necropoleis: Report on the researches at Erganos, Panaghia, and Courtes. *American Journal of Archaeology* 5(3): 259–293. https://doi.org/10.2307/496700.

Halbherr, F. and Orsi, P. (1888). Scoperte nell'antro di Psychrò. *Museo italiano di antichità classica* 2: 905–910.

Hamilakis, Y. (2002). What future for the 'Minoan' past? Rethinking Minoan archaeology. In Y. Hamilakis, ed., *Labyrinth Revisited: Rethinking 'Minoan' Archaeology*. Oxford: Oxbow Books, pp. 2–28.

Hamilakis, Y. (2007). *The Nation and its Ruins: Antiquity, Archaeology, and National Imagination in Greece*. Oxford: Oxford University Press.

Hamilakis, Y. (2008). Decolonizing Greek Archaeology: Indigenous Archaeologies, Modernist Archaeology, and the Post-colonial Critique. In D. Damaskos and D. Plantzos, eds., A Singular Antiquity: Archaeology and Hellenic Identity in Twentieth-Century Greece. Athens: The Benaki Museum, pp. 273–284.

Hamilakis, Y. (2011). Indigenous archaeologies in Ottoman Greece. In Z. Bahrani, Z. Celik and E. Eldem, eds., *Scramble for the Past: The Story of Archaeology in the Ottoman Empire*. Istanbul: SALT, pp. 49–69.

Hamilakis, Y. and Momigliano, N. (2006). Archaeology and European modernity: Stories from the borders. In Y. Hamilakis and N. Momigliano, eds., *Archaeology and European Modernity: Producing and Consuming the 'Minoans'*. Padua: Bottega d'Erasmo, pp. 25–35.

Hatzidakis, I. (1921). *Tylissos à l'époque minoenne, suivi d'une note sur les larnax de Tylissos*. Paris: P. Geuthner.

Hatzidakis, I. (1931). *Ιστορία του Κρητικού Μουσείου και των αρχαιολογικών ερευνών εν Κρήτη*. Athens: Archaeological Society at Athens.

Haussoullier, B. (1880). Vases peints archaïques découverts à Cnossos (Crète). *Revue Archéologique* 40: 359–361.

Hawes, H. B. (1908). *Gournia, Vasiliki and other Prehistoric Sites on the Isthmus of Hierapetra, Crete*. Philadelphia: The American Exploration Society.

Hawes, C. H. and Hawes, H. B. (1911). *Crete, the Forerunner of Greece*. 2nd ed. New York: Harper & Brothers.

Heurtley, W. A. (1939). *Prehistoric Macedonia*. Cambridge: Cambridge University Press.

Heurtley, W. A. and Lorimer, H. L. (1933). Excavations in Ithaca, I. LH III: Protogeometric cairns at Aetós. *Annual of the British School at Athens* 33: 22–65. https://doi.org/10.1017/S0068245400011825.

Heuzey, L. (1860). *Le Mont Olympe et L'Acarnanie*. Paris: Firmin Didot Frères.

Hielte, M. (2023). Aphidna's prehistoric tumulus in North Attica from around 2000 BC. A comprehensive re-assessment of Sam Wide's 1894 excavation. *Acta Archaeologica* 92(2): 277–331. https://doi.org/10.1163/16000390-20210033.

Hitchcock, L. and Koudounaris, P. (2002). Virtual discourse: Arthur Evans and the reconstructions of the Minoan palace at Knossos. In Y. Hamilakis, ed., *Labyrinth Revisited: Rethinking 'Minoan' Archaeology*. Oxford: Oxbow Books, pp. 40–58.

Hoeck, K. F. C. (1823–29). *Kreta, I–III*. Göttingen: Rosenbusch.

Hogarth, D. G. (1900a). Knossos. Summary report of the excavations in 1900: II. Early town and cemeteries. *Annual of the British School at Athens* 6: 70–85. https://doi.org/10.1017/S006824540000191X.

Hogarth, D. G. (1900b). The Dictaean Cave. *Annual of the British School at Athens* 6: 94–116. https://doi.org/10.1017/S0068245400001945.

Hogarth, D. G. (1901). Excavations at Zakro, Crete. *Annual of the British School at Athens* 7: 121–149. https://doi.org/10.1017/S0068245400001283.

Hogarth, D. G. (1910). *Accidents of an Antiquary's Life*. London: Macmillan.

Hood, S. and Taylor, W. (1981). *The Bronze Age Palace at Knossos: Plan and Sections*. London: British School at Athens.

Horejs, B. (2014). The 2nd millennium BC in the Bakircay (Kaykos) Valley: An overview. In N. Çınardalı Karaaslan, A. Aykurt, N. Kolankaya-Bostancı, and Y. H. Erbil, eds., *Anadolu Kültürlerine Bir Bakış. Armağan Erkanal'a Armağan/ Some Observation on Anatolian Cultures. Compiled in Honor of Armağan Erkanal*. Ankara: Hacettepe University Press, pp. 257–274.

Horwitz, S. L. (1981). *The Find of a Lifetime: Sir Arthur Evans and the Discovery of Knossos*. London: Weidenfeld & Nicolson.

Hughey, J. R., Paschou, P., Drineas, P., et al. (2013). A European population in Minoan Bronze Age Crete. *Nature Communications* 4(1): 1861. https://doi.org/10.1038/ncomms2871.

Huxley, D. (2000). *Cretan Quests: British Explorers, Excavators and Historians*. Athens: British School at Athens.

Iakovidis, S. and French, E. B. (2003). The excavated areas within the citadel. In S. Iakovidis and E. B. French, eds., *Archaeological Atlas of Mycenae*. Athens: Archaeological Society at Athens, pp. 10–18.

Inglieri, R. (1936). *Carta Archaeologica dell'Isola di Rodi*. Florence: R. Instituto Geografico Militare.

Jacopi, G. (1931). Nuovi Scavi nella Necropoli Micenea di Jalisso. *Annuario della Regia scuola archeologica di Atene e delle missioni italiane in Oriente* 13–14: 253–345.

Karadimas, N. (2015). The unknown past of Minoan archaeology: From the Renaissance until the arrival of Sir Arthur Evans in Crete. In S. Cappel, U. Günkel-Maschek and D. Panagiotopoulos, eds., *Minoan Archaeology: Perspectives for the 21st Century*. Louvain-la-Neuve: Presses universitaires de Louvain, pp. 3–15.

Karadimas, N. and Momigliano, N. (2004). On the term 'Minoan' before Evans's work in Crete (1894). *Studi Micenei ed Egeo-Anatolici* 46: 243–258.

Karo, G. (1930). *Die Schachtgräber von Mykenai*. Munich: Bruckmann.

Kavvadias, P. (1912). Περί των εν Κεφαλληνία ανασκαφών. *Πρακτικά της εν Αθήναις Αρχαιολογικής Εταιρείας* 67: 247–268.

Keramopoullos, A. (1909). Η οικία του Κάδμου. *Αρχαιολογική Εφημερίς* 1909: 57–122.

Köhler, U. (1884). Praehistorisches von den griechischen Inseln. *Mitteilungen des Deutschen Archäologischen Instituts, Athenische Abteilung* 9: 156–162.

Kokkou, A. (1977). *Η μέριμνα για τις αρχαιότητες στην Ελλάδα και τα πρώτα μουσεία*. Athens: Ermis.

Kondakis, I. and Kastorchis, E. (1878). Περί των πάρα την Ναυπλίαν πανάρχαιων τάφων. *Athenaion* 7: 183–201.

Konstantinidi-Syvridi, E. and Paschalidis, K. (2019). The unacknowledged Panayotis Stamatakis and his invaluable contribution to the understanding of Grave Circle A at Mycenae. *Archaeological Reports* 65: 111–126. https://doi.org/10.1017/S0570608419000061.

Kopaka, K. (2015). Minos Kalokairinos and his early excavation at Knossos: An overview, a portrait and a return to the Kefala pithoi. In C. Macdonald, E. Hatzaki and S. Andreou, eds., *The Great Islands: Studies of Crete and Cyprus Presented to Gerald Cadogan*. Athens: Kapon Editions, pp. 143–151.

Korka, E., ed. (2007). *Foreign Archaeological Schools in Greece from the 19th to the 21st Century*. Athens: Hellenic Ministry of Culture.

Kotsakis, K. (2017). Trenches, borders and boundaries: Prehistoric research in Greek Macedonia. In A. J. Shapland and E. Stefani, eds., *Archaeology behind the Battle Lines: The Macedonian Campaign (1915–19) and Its Legacy*. London: Routledge, pp. 58–68.

Kotsonas, A. (2018). A cultural history of the Cretan Labyrinth: Monument and memory from prehistory to the present. *American Journal of Archaeology* 122(3): 367–396. https://doi.org/10.3764/aja.122.3.0367.

Koumanoudis, S. and Kastorchis, E. (1877). Οι εν Σπάτα Αττικής αρχαίοι τάφοι. *Athenaion* 6: 167–172.

Kourouniotis, K. (1906). Ανασκαφή θολωτού τάφου εν Βόλω. *Αρχαιολογική Εφημερίς* 1906: 211–240.

Kourtessi-Philippakis, G. (2006). Chasseurs-cueilleurs paléolithiques dans le monde égéen: veut-on de ces ancêtres? In P. Darcque, M. Fotiadis and O. Polychronopoulou, eds., *Mythos: la préhistoire égéenne du XIXe au XXIe siècle après J.-C*. Athens: École Française d'Athènes, pp. 245–256.

Krzyszkowska, O. (2005). *Aegean Seals: An Introduction*. London: Institute of Classical Studies.

La Rosa, V. (2012a). Ayia Triada. In E. H. Cline, ed., *The Oxford Handbook of the Bronze Age Aegean*. Oxford: Oxford University Press, pp. 496–508.

La Rosa, V. (2012b). Phaistos. In E. H. Cline, ed., *The Oxford Handbook of the Bronze Age Aegean*. Oxford: Oxford University Press, pp. 582–596.

La Rosa, V. and Rizzo, M. A., eds. (1985). *Ancient Crete. A Hundred Years of Italian Archaeology (1884–1984)*. Rome: De Luca Editore.

Laffineur, R. and Perna, M., eds. (2024). *IXNH. Walking in the Footsteps of the Pioneer of Aegean Archaeology in Celebration of the 200th Anniversary of the Birth of Heinrich Schliemann*. Leuven: Peeters.

Lamb, W. (1936). *Excavations at Thermi in Lesbos*. Cambridge: Cambridge University Press.

Lamb, W. and Wace, A. J. B. (1921). Excavations at Mycenae. *Annual of the British School at Athens* 24: 185–209.

Lane, M. F. (2021). Gla. *Oxford Classical Dictionary*. Oxford: Oxford University Press. https://doi.org/10.1093/acrefore/9780199381135.013.2844.

Lavery, J. and French, E. B. (2003). Early accounts of Mycenae. In S. Iakovidis and E. B. French, eds., *Archaeological Atlas of Mycenae*. Athens: Archaeological Society at Athens, pp. 1–4.

Lazaridis, I., Mittnik, A., Patterson, N., et al. (2017). Genetic origins of the Minoans and Mycenaeans. *Nature* 548(7666): 214–218. https://doi.org/10.1038/nature23310.

Leake, W. M. (1830). *Travels in the Morea, II*. London: John Murray.

Leake, W. M. (1835). *Travels in Northern Greece, IV*. London: J. Rodwell.

Lechevalier, J.-B. (1799). *Voyage dans la Troade, ou Tableau de la plaine de Troie dans son etat actuel*. 2nd ed. France: Chez Laran.

Lee, J. (1849). Antiquarian researches in the Ionian Islands, in the year 1812. *Archaeologia* 33: 36–54. https://doi.org/10.1017/S0261340900000047.

Lenormant, F. (1866). Découverte de constructions antéhistoriques dans l'île de Therasia. *Revue Archéologique* 14: 423–432.

Lolling, H. G. (1880). *Das Kuppelgrab bei Menidi*. Athens: Deutsches Archäologisches Institut.

Lolling, H. G. and Wolters, P. (1886). Das Kuppelgrab bei Dimini. *Mitteilungen des Deutschen Archäologischen Instituts, Athenische Abteilung* 11: 435–443.

Long, C. R. (1974). *The Ayia Triadha Sarcophagus, a Study of Late Minoan and Mycenaean Funerary Practices and Beliefs*. Gothenburg: Paul Åströms Förlag.

Lubbock, J. (1865). *Pre-Historic Times*. London: Williams & Norgate.

Ludwig, E. (1931). *Schliemann of Troy: The Story of a Goldseeker*. London: G. P. Putnam's sons.

Mac Sweeney, N. (2018). *Troy: Myth, City, Icon*. London: Bloomsbury.

MacGillivray, J. A. (2000). *Minotaur: Sir Arthur Evans and the Archaeology of the Minoan Myth*. London: Jonathan Cape.

MacKendrick, P. (1962). *The Greek Stones Speak: The Story of Archaeology in Greek Lands*. London: Methuen.

Mackenzie, D. (1904). The successive settlements at Phylakopi in their Aegeo-Cretan relations. In T. D. Atkinson, R. C. Bosanquet, and C. C. Edgar, eds., *Excavations at Phylakopi in Melos*. London: Society for the Promotion of Hellenic Studies, pp. 238–272.

Maclaren, C. (1822). *A Dissertation on the Topography of the Plain of Troy*. Edinburgh: Constable.

Maclaren, C. (1863). *The Plain of Troy Described and the Identity of the Ilium of Homer with the Ilium Novum of Strabo Proved*. Edinburgh: Black.

Macmillan, G. A. (1911). A short history of the British School at Athens, 1886–1911. *Annual of the British School at Athens* 17: ix–xxxviii. https://doi.org/10.1017/S0068245400008352.

Maiuri, A. (1926). Jalisos: Scavi della Missione Archeological Italiana a Rodi. Parte 1: La Necropoli Micenea. *Annuario della Regia scuola archeologica di Atene e delle missioni italiane in Oriente* 6–7: 86–256.

Mandalaki, S. (2023). The Minoan legacy of the Heraklion Archaeological Museum. In A. J. Shapland, ed., *Labyrinth: Knossos, Myth & Reality*. Oxford: Ashmolean Museum, pp. 29–33.

Maran, J. (2016). The persistence of place and memory: The case of the Early Helladic Rundbau and the Mycenaean palatial megara of Tiryns. In M. Bartelheim, B. Horejs and R. Krauss, eds., *Von Baden bis Troia: Ressourcennutzung, Metallurgie und Wissenstransfer. Eine Jubiläumsschrift für Ernst Pernicka*. Rahden/Westf.: Marie Leidorf, pp. 153–173.

Marinatos, N. (2014). *Sir Arthur Evans and Minoan Crete: Creating the Vision of Knossos*. London: Bloomsbury.

Marinatos, S. (1939). The volcanic destruction of Minoan Crete. *Antiquity* 13(52): 425–439. https://doi.org/10.1017/S0003598X00028088.

Marthari, M. (1998). *Syros, Chalandriani-Kastri: From the Investigation and Protection to the Presentation of an Archaeological Site*. Athens: Ministry of Culture.

Matz, F., ed. (1951). *Forschungen auf Kreta 1942*. Berlin: De Gruyter.

McDonald, W. (1967). *Progress into the Past: The Re-discovery of Mycenaean Civilisation*. New York: Macmillan.

McNeal, R. A. (1973). The legacy of Arthur Evans. *California Studies in Classical Antiquity* 6: 205–220.

McNeal, R. A. (1975). Helladic Prehistory through the looking-glass. *Historia: Zeitschrift für Alte Geschichte* 24(3): 385–401.

Mee, C. (1982). *Rhodes in the Bronze Age: An Archaeological Survey*. Warminster: Aris & Phillips.

Meyer, E. (1958). *Heinrich Schliemann: Briefwechsel, II*. Berlin: Mann.

Milchhöfer, A. (1883). *Die Anfänge der Kunst in Griechenland*. Leipzig: Brockhaus.

Momigliano, N. (1999). *Duncan Mackenzie: A Cautious Canny Highlander and the Palace of Minos at Knossos*. London: Institute of Classical Studies.

Moore, D., Rowlands, E. and Karadimas, N. (2014). *In Search of Agamemnon: Early Travellers to Mycenae*. Newcastle upon Tyne: Cambridge Scholars Publishing.

Morris, I. (1994). Archaeologies of Greece. In I. Morris, ed., *Classical Greece: Ancient Histories and Modern Archaeologies*. Cambridge: Cambridge University Press, pp. 8–48.

Moshenska, G. and Lewis, C. (2023). Introduction. In C. Lewis and G. Moshenska, eds., *Life-Writing in the History of Archaeology: Critical Perspectives*. London: UCL Press, pp. 1–22.

Muhly, J. D., ed. (2000). *One Hundred Years of American Archaeological Work on Crete*. Athens: American School of Classical Studies at Athens/INSTAP Study Center for East Crete.

Müller, F. M. (1856). *Comparative Mythology: An Essay*. London: Routledge.

Müller, K. O. (1820). *Orchomenos und die Minyer*. Breslau: Josef Mar.

Müller, K. O. (1824). *Die Dorier*. Breslau: Josef Mar.

Myres, J. N. L. (1933). The Cretan Labyrinth: A retrospect of Aegean research. The Huxley Memorial Lecture for 1933. *Journal of the Royal Anthropological Institute of Great Britain and Ireland* 63: 269–312.

Neumeier, E. (2017). Rivaling Elgin: Ottoman governors and archaeological agency in the Morea. In B. Anderson and F. Rojas, eds., *Antiquarianisms: Contact, Conflict, and Comparison*. Oxford: Oxbow Books, pp. 134–160.

Newton, C. T. (1865). *Travels and Discoveries in the Levant*. London: Day & Son.

Newton, C. T. (1880). Dr. Schliemann's Discoveries at Mycenae. In C. Newton, ed., *Essays on Art and Archaeology*. London: Macmillan, pp. 246–302.

Orlandi, L. (2022). Searching for 'Italianità' in the Dodecanese Islands (1912–1943). Some considerations on art, architecture and archaeology through the works of Hermes Balducci. In B. Falcucci, E. Giusti and D. Trentacoste, eds., *Rereading Travellers to the East: Shaping Identities and Building the Nation in Post-unification Italy*. Florence: Firenze University Press, pp. 125–140.

Özkaya, B. T. (2022). Entangled geographies, contested narratives: The Canning Marbles and the Ottoman response to Antiquity. *Muqarnas* 39: 227–254.

Palli, O. (2012). The Toumba of Thessaloniki. In P. Adam-Veleni and A. Koukouvou, eds., *Archaeology behind Battle Lines, Thessaloniki of the Turbulent Years 1912–1922*. Thessaloniki: Archaeological Museum of Thessaloniki, pp. 98–103.

Panagiotaki, M. (2004). Knossos objects: 1904, the first departure. In G. Cadogan, E. Hatzaki and A. Vasilakis, eds., *Knossos: Palace, City, State*. London: British School at Athens, pp. 565–580.

Papadimitriou, N., Philippa-Touchais, A. and Touchais, G. (2020). The Mycenaean cemetery of Deiras, Argos, in a local and regional context. In

J. M. A. Murphy, ed., *Death in Late Bronze Age Greece*. Oxford: Oxford University Press, pp. 60–88.

Papadopoulos, J. (2005). Inventing the Minoans: Archaeology, modernity and the quest for European identity. *Journal of Mediterranean Archaeology* 18(1): 87–149. https://doi.org/10.1558/jmea.2005.18.1.87.

Papazoglou-Manioudaki, L. (2017). The Early Cycladic figurines from the excavations of Clon Stephanos on Syros and a note on his work on Naxos: Towards context. In M. Marthari, C. Renfrew and M. Boyd, eds., *Early Cycladic Sculpture in Context*. Oxford: Oxbow, pp. 310–334.

Papazoglou-Manioudaki, L., Nafplioti, A., Musgrave, J. H., et al. (2009). Mycenae revisited Part 1. The human remains from Grave Circle A: Stamatakis, Schliemann and two new faces from Shaft Grave VI. *Annual of the British School at Athens* 104: 233–277. https://doi.org/10.1017/S0068245400000241.

Pashley, R. (1837). *Travels in Crete, II*. London: John Murray.

Paton, W. R. (1887). Vases from Calymnos and Carpathos. *Journal of Hellenic Studies* 8: 446–460.

Payne Knight, R. (1809). *Specimens of ancient sculpture: Ægyptian, Etruscan, Greek, and Roman*. London: T. Payne & J. White.

Pelon, O., Andersen, E. and Olivier, J.-P. (1980). *Le Palais de Malia. V*. Paris: P. Geuthner.

Pernier, L. (1935). *Il palazzo minoico di Festòs: scavi e studi della Missione archeologica italiana a Creta dal 1900 al 1934, I*. Rome: Libreria Dello Stato.

Pernier, L. and Banti, L. (1951). *Il palazzo minoico di Festòs: scavi e studi della Missione archeologica italiana a Creta dal 1900 a 1950, II*. Rome: Libreria Dello Stato.

Perrot, G. and Chipiez, C. (1894a). *History of Art in Primitive Greece, I*. London: Chapman and Hall.

Perrot, G. and Chipiez, C. (1894b). *History of Art in Primitive Greece, II*. London: Chapman and Hall.

Persson, A. W. (1931). *The Royal Tombs at Dendra near Midea*. Lund: Gleerup.

Persson, A. W. (1942). *New Tombs at Dendra near Midea*. Lund: Gleerup.

Petrakos, V. (1987). *Η εν Αθήναις Αρχαιολογική Εταιρεία: η ιστορία των 150 χρόνων της, 1837–1987*. Athens: Archaeological Society at Athens.

Petrakos, V. (2009). *Η ελληνική αυταπάτη του Λουδοβίκου Ross*. Athens: Archaeological Society at Athens.

Petrie, W. M. F. (1890). The Egyptian bases of Greek history. *Journal of Hellenic Studies* 11: 271–277. https://doi.org/10.2307/623432.

Petrie, W. M. F. (1891). Notes on the antiquities of Mycenae. *Journal of Hellenic Studies* 12: 199–205. https://doi.org/10.2307/623511.

Petrochilos, J. E. (1992). *Βαλέριος Στάης*. Athens: Archaeological Society at Athens.

Phillips, J. (2006). Petrie, the 'outsider looking in'. In P. Darcque, M. Fotiadis and O. Polychronopoulou, eds., *Mythos: la préhistoire égéenne du XIXe au XXIe siècle après J.-C*. Athens: Ecole française d'Athènes, pp. 143–157.

Pryce, F. N. (1928). *A Catalogue of Sculpture in the Department of Greek and Roman Antiquities, British Museum, I,I*. London: Trustees of the British Museum.

Renfrew, A. C. (1969). The development and chronology of the Early Cycladic figurines. *American Journal of Archaeology* 73: 1–32. https://doi.org/10.2307/503370.

Renfrew, A. C. (1972). *The Emergence of Civilisation*. London: Methuen.

Rennell Rodd, J. (1933). The Ithaca of the Odyssey. *Annual of the British School at Athens* 33: 1–21.

Rey, L. (1919). Observations sur les premieres habitats de la Macédoine. *Bulletin de Correspondance Hellénique* 41–43: 1–310.

Ridgeway, W. (1901). *The Early Age of Greece, I*. Cambridge: Cambridge University Press.

Rose, C. B. (2013). *The Archaeology of Greek and Roman Troy*. Cambridge: Cambridge University Press.

Ross, L. (1837). Über Anaphe und Anaphäische Inschriften. *Abhandlungen der Philosophisch-Philologischen Classe der Königlich Bayerischen Akademie der Wissenschaften* 2: 399–450.

Ross, L. (1840). *Reisen auf den griechischen Inseln des ägäischen Meeres*. Stuttgart: Cotta.

Runnels, C. (2008). George Finlay's contributions to the discovery of the Stone Age in Greece. *Annual of the British School at Athens* 103: 9–25. https://doi.org/10.1017/S0068245400000058.

Salmon, N. (2018). Excavation and documentation of the Rhodian countryside and Dodecanese islands in the first millennium BC. *Archaeological Reports* 65: 157–175. https://doi.org/10.1017/S0570608419000097.

Salmon, N. (2019). Archives and attribution: Reconstructing the British Museum's excavation of Kamiros. In S. Schierup, ed., *Documenting Ancient Rhodes. Proceedings of an International Conference held at the National Museum of Denmark, 16–17 February 2017*. Aarhus: Aarhus University Press, pp. 98–112.

Sandars, N. K. (1963). Later Aegean bronze swords. *American Journal of Archaeology* 67(2): 117–153. https://doi.org/10.2307/502611.

Savino, M. (2012). Narrating the 'New' History: Museums in the construction of the Turkish Republic. In D. Poulot, F. Bodenstein and J. L. Guiral, eds., *Great Narratives of the Past. Traditions and Revisions in National Museums*. Linköping: LiU E-Press, pp. 253–264.

Sayce, A. (1880). The inscriptions found at Hissarlik. In H. Schliemann, ed., *Ilios: The City and Country of the Trojans*. London: John Murray, pp. 691–705.

Schiering, W. (2010). Tiryns (CT). In H. Cancik, M. Chase, F. G. Gentry, M. Landfester, and H. Schneider, eds., *Brill's New Pauly, V.* Leiden: Brill, pp. 567–578.

Schliemann, H. (1869). *Ithaque, Le Péloponnèse, Troie: Recherches Archéo logiques*. France: C. Reinwald.

Schliemann, H. (1874). *Atlas trojanischer Alterthümer: Photographische Berichte über die Ausgrabungen in Troja*. Leipzig: F. A. Brockhaus.

Schliemann, H. (1875). *Troy and its Remains: A Narrative of Researches and Discoveries made on the Site of Ilium, and in the Trojan Plain*. England: John Murray.

Schliemann, H. (1878). *Mycenae: A Narrative of Researches and Discoveries at Mycenae and Tiryns*. London: John Murray.

Schliemann, H. (1880). *Ilios: The City and Country of the Trojans*. London: John Murray.

Schliemann, H. (1881a). Exploration of the Boeotian Orchomenus. *Journal of Hellenic Studies* 2: 122–163. https://doi.org/10.2307/623560.

Schliemann, H. (1881b). *Orchomenos: Bericht über meine Ausgrabungen im böotischen Orchomenos*. Leipzig: Brockhaus.

Schliemann, H. (1885). *Tiryns: The Prehistoric Palace of the Kings of Tiryns*. London: John Murray.

Schmidt, H. (1902a). Die Keramik der makedonischen Tumuli. *Zeitschrift für Ethnologie* 34: 76–77.

Schmidt, H. (1902b). *Heinrich Schliemann's Sammlung trojanischer Altertümer*. Berlin: G. Reimer.

Schnapp, A. (1996). *The Discovery of the Past: The Origins of Archaeology*. London: British Museum Press.

Schoep, I. (2018). Building the Labyrinth: Arthur Evans and the construction of Minoan civilization. *American Journal of Archaeology* 122(1): 5–32. https://doi.org/10.3764/aja.122.1.0005.

Schuchhardt, C. (1891). *Schliemann's Excavations: An Archaeological and Historical Study*. London: Macmillan.

Seager, R. B. (1910). *Excavations on the Island of Pseira, Crete*. Pennsylvania: The University Museum.

Seager, R. B. (1912). *Explorations in the Island of Mochlos*. Massachusetts: American School of Classical Studies at Athens.

Sergi, G. (1901a). Cretan Expedition XIV. Notes upon the skulls of Erganos. *American Journal of Archaeology* 5(3): 315–318. https://doi.org/10.2307/496703.

Sergi, G. (1901b). *The Mediterranean Race: A Study of the Origin of European Peoples*. London: Walter Scott.

Shapland, A. J. and Stefani, E., eds. (2017). *Archaeology behind the Battle Lines: The Macedonian Campaign (1915–19) and its Legacy*. London: Routledge.

Shaw, W. M. K. (2003). *Possessors and Possessed: Museums, Archaeology, and the Visualization of History in the Late Ottoman Empire*. Berkeley: University of California Press.

Smith, A. H. (1892). *A Catalogue of Archaic Greek Sculpture in the British Museum*. London: Trustees of the British Museum.

Soteriadis, G. (1908). Προϊστορικά αγγεία Χαιρώνειας και Ελατείας. *Αρχαιολογική Εφημερίς* 1908: 63–96.

Souyoudzoglou-Haywood, C. (1999). *The Ionian Islands in the Bronze Age and Early Iron Age, 3000–800 BC*. Liverpool: Liverpool University Press.

Souyoudzoglou-Haywood, C. (2018). Archaeology and the search for Homeric Ithaca: The case of Mycenaean Kephalonia. *Acta Archaeologica* 89(1): 145–158. https://doi.org/10.1111/j.1600-0390.2018.12197.x.

Spon, J. and Wheler, G. (1678). *Voyage d'Italie, de Dalmatie, de Grèce et du Levant: fait aux années 1675 et 1676*. Lyon: Antoine Cellier.

Spratt, T. A. B. (1865). *Travels and Researches in Crete, I–II*. London: John van Voorst.

Stamatakis, P. (1878). Περί του παρά το Ηραίον καθαρισθέντος τάφου. *Mitteilungen des Deutschen Archäologischen Instituts, Athenische Abteilung* 2: 271–286.

Stefani, E. and Shapland, A. J. (forthcoming). Aegean prehistory in the wake of Venizelos: Crete and Macedonia. In S. Triantaphyllou, K. Efkleidou and L. Vokotopoulos, eds., *Stellar Ventures*. Philadelphia: INSTAP Academic Press.

Stillman, W. (1881). Extracts from letters of W.J. Stillman, respecting ancient sites in Crete. In *American Institute of Archaeology: Second Annual Report of the Executive Committee, 1880–81*. Cambridge, MA: John Wilson, pp. 41–49.

Stubbings, F. H. (1972). *Prehistoric Greece*. London: Hart-Davis.

Taramelli, A. (1897). Cretan Expedition VIII. The prehistoric grotto at Miamù. *American Journal of Archaeology* 1(4/5): 287–312. https://doi.org/10.2307/496717.

Taramelli, A. (1901a). Cretan Expedition XIX. A Visit to Phaestos. *American Journal of Archaeology* 5(4): 418–436. https://doi.org/10.2307/496584.

Taramelli, A. (1901b). Cretan Expedition XX. A visit to the Grotto of Camares on Mount Ida. *American Journal of Archaeology* 5(4): 437–451. https://doi.org/10.2307/496585.

Tartaron, T. F. (2004). *Bronze Age Landscape and Society in Southern Epirus, Greece.* Oxford: BAR Publishing.

Thiersch, F. (1835). Über Paros und parischen Inschriften *Abhandlungen der Philosophisch-Philologischen Classe der Königlich Bayerischen Akademie der Wissenschaften* 1: 583–644.

Thomas, J. (2004). *Archaeology and Modernity.* London: Routledge.

Traeger, P. (1902). Die macedonischen Tumuli und ihre Keramik. *Zeitschrift für Ethnologie* 34: 62–76.

Traill, D. A. (1995). *Schliemann of Troy: Treasure and Deceit.* London: John Murray.

Trigger, B. G. (1989). *A History of Archaeological Thought.* Cambridge: Cambridge University Press.

Tsountas, C. (1888). Ανασκαφαί Μηκηνών του 1886. *Πρακτικά της εν Αθήναις Αρχαιολογικής Εταιρείας* 1886: 59–79.

Tsountas, C. (1889). Έρευναι εν τη Λακωνική και ο τάφος του Βαφειού. *Αρχαιολογική Εφημερίς* 1889: 129–172.

Tsountas, C. (1893). *Μυκήναι και Μυκηναίος Πολιτισμός.* Athens: Hestia.

Tsountas, C. (1898). Κυκλαδικά I. *Αρχαιολογική Εφημερίς* 1898: 137–212.

Tsountas, C. (1899). Κυκλαδικά II. *Αρχαιολογική Εφημερίς* 1899: 73–134.

Tsountas, C. (1908). *Αί προϊστορικαί ακροπόλεις Διμηνίου και Σέσκλου.* Athens: Archaeological Society at Athens.

Tsountas, C. and Manatt, J. I. (1897). *The Mycenaean Age: A Study of the Monuments and Culture of Pre-Homeric Greece.* London: Macmillan.

Tzachili, I. (2005). Excavations on Thera and Therasia in the 19th century: A chronicle. *Journal of Mediterranean Archaeology* 18(2): 231–257. https://doi.org/10.1558/jmea.2005.18.2.231.

Tzonou-Herbst, I. (2015). From the mud of Peirene to mastering stratigraphy: Carl Blegen in the Corinthia and Argolid. In N. Vogeikoff-Brogan, J. L. Davis and V. Florou, eds., *Carl W. Blegen: Personal and Archaeological Narratives.* Atlanta: Lockwood Press, pp. 39–62.

Varouchakis, V. (2017). Indigenous Archaeologies of Crete, 1878–1913. *Public Archaeology* 16(1): 42–66. https://doi.org/10.1080/14655187.2017.1431100.

Vickers, M. J. (2006). *The Arundel and Pomfret Marbles in Oxford*. Oxford: Ashmolean Museum.

Vollgraff, W. (1904). Fouilles d'Argos. *Bulletin de Correspondance Hellénique* 28: 364–399.

Voudouri, D. (2008). Greek legislation concerning the international movement of antiquities and its ideological and political dimensions. In D. Damaskos and D. Plantzos, eds., *A Singular Antiquity: Archaeology and Hellenic Identity in Twentieth-Century Greece*. Athens: Benaki Museum, pp. 125–139.

Voudouri, D. (2017). The legal protection of antiquities in Greece and national identity. In S. Voutsaki and P. Cartledge, eds., *Ancient Monuments and Modern Identities: A History of Archaeology in 19th and 20th Century Greece*. London: Routledge, pp. 77–94.

Voutsaki, S. (2002). The 'Greekness' of Greek prehistory: An investigation of the debate 1876–1900. *Pharos* 10: 105–122.

Voutsaki, S. (2017). The Hellenization of Greek prehistory: The work of Christos Tsountas. In S. Voutsaki and P. Cartledge, eds., *Ancient Monuments and Modern Identities: A History of Archaeology in 19th and 20th Century Greece*. London: Routledge, pp. 130–147.

Wace, A. J. B. (1914). The mounds of Macedonia. *Annual of the British School at Athens* 20: 123–132. https://doi.org/10.1017/S0068245400009448.

Wace, A. J. B. and Blegen, C. W. (1918). The pre-Mycenaean pottery of the mainland. *Annual of the British School at Athens* 22: 175–189. https://doi.org/10.1017/S0068245400009916.

Wace, A. J. B. and Thompson, M. S. (1909). Prehistoric mounds in Macedonia. *Annals of Archaeology and Anthropology* 2: 159–164.

Wace, A. J. B. and Thompson, M. S. (1912). *Prehistoric Thessaly*. Cambridge: Cambridge University Press.

Wace, A. J. B., Heurtley, W. A., Lamb, W., Holland, L. B., and Boethius, C. A. (1923). The Report of the School Excavations at Mycenae, 1921–1923. *Annual of the British School at Athens* 25: 1–434.

Waldstein, C. (1902–1905). *The Argive Heraeum, I–II*. Boston: Houghton Mifflin.

Warren, P. (2000). Sir Arthur Evans and his achievement. *Bulletin of the Institute of Classical Studies* 44(1): 199–211. https://doi.org/10.1111/j.2041-5370.2000.tb00604.x.

Waterhouse, H. (1986). *British School at Athens: The First Hundred Years*. London: Thames & Hudson.

Welch, F. B. (1919). Macedonia. III. Prehistoric Pottery. *Annual of the British School at Athens* 23: 44–50. https://doi.org/10.1017/S0068245400003683.

Whitley, J. (2007). British School at Athens. In E. Korka, ed., *Foreign Archaeological Schools in Greece from the 19th to the 21st Century*. Athens: Hellenic Ministry of Culture, pp. 62–75.

Whitley, J. (2024). *Knossos: Myth, History and Archaeology*. London: Bloomsbury.

Wide, S. (1896). Aphidna in Nordattika. *Mitteilungen des Deutschen Archäologischen Instituts, Athenische Abteilung* 21: 385–409.

Wolf, F. A. (1795). *Prolegomena ad Homerum*. Halle: Libraria Orphanotrophei.

Wolters, P. (1889). Mykenische Vasen aus dem nördlichen Griechenland *Mitteilungen des Deutschen Archäologischen Instituts, Athenische Abteilung* 14: 262–270.

Wood, R. (1775). *Essay on the Original Genius and Writings of Homer with a Comparative View of the Ancient and Present State of the Troade*. London: T. Payne.

Xanthoudides, S. A. (1924). *The Vaulted Tombs of Mesara: An Account of Some Early Cemeteries of Southern Crete*. London: Hodder & Stoughton.

Zervos, C. (1957). *L'Art des Cyclades*. Paris: Éditions 'Cahiers d'Art'.

Acknowledgements

With thanks to Carl Knappett and Irene Nikolakopoulou for commissioning this Element and for their advice and support during its production. I would also like to thank two anonymous reviewers, Nico Momigliano and Susanna Shapland for their helpful comments on drafts of the manuscript. A sabbatical from the Ashmolean Museum enabled me to complete the research underpinning this work. I would also like to thank the staff of the Art, Archaeology and Ancient World Library in Oxford for their help.

Cambridge Elements

The Aegean Bronze Age

Carl Knappett
University of Toronto
Carl Knappett is the Walter Graham/ Homer Thompson Chair in Aegean Prehistory at the University of Toronto.

Irene Nikolakopoulou
Hellenic Ministry of Culture, Archaeological Museum of Heraklion
Irene Nikolakopoulou is an archaeologist and curator at the Archaeological Museum of Heraklion, Crete.

About the Series
This series is devised thematically to foreground the conceptual developments in the Aegean Bronze Age, one of the richest subfields of archaeology, while reflecting the range of institutional settings in which research in this field is conducted. It aims to produce an innovative and comprehensive review of the latest scholarship in Aegean prehistory.

Cambridge Elements

The Aegean Bronze Age

Elements in the Series

Long-Distance Exchange and Inter-Regional Economies
Sarah C. Murray

Aegeomania: Modern Reimaginings of the Aegean Bronze Age
Nicoletta Momigliano

Economy and Commodity Production in the Aegean Bronze Age
Catherine E. Pratt

The Emergence of Aegean Prehistory
Andrew Shapland

A full series listing is available at: www.cambridge.org/EABA

For EU product safety concerns, contact us at Calle de José Abascal, 56–1°, 28003 Madrid, Spain or eugpsr@cambridge.org.

www.ingramcontent.com/pod-product-compliance
Lightning Source LLC
LaVergne TN
LVHW020349260326
834688LV00045B/1623